CHOCOLATE CHIP SWEETS

For Benjamin and Marki, Danny, Michael, Willie, and Mary Rose,

Love

who ate all the chips.

CHOCOLATE CHIP SWEETS

FAVORITE RECIPES FROM CELEBRATED CHEFS

TRACEY ZABAR

PHOTOGRAPHY BY ELLEN SILVERMAN

RIZZOLI
NEW YORK

New York · Paris · London · Milan

CONTENTS

I am crazy for chocolate chips. And I'm not alone. People can't get enough of these sweet add-ins. They are the classic addition to everyone's favorite cookie, which is quintessentially more American than apple pie. Ever since Mrs. Ruth Graves Wakefield famously dropped a chopped bar of chocolate into her cookie batter and invented the iconic Toll House Cookies, named after her inn in Whitman, Massachusetts, dessert aficionados have been clamoring for them. They are chewy and crunchy, filled with slightly melted chocolate bits. These scrumptious cookies should be savored warm from the oven with a glass of cold milk or dressed up by sandwiching ice cream in the middle or crumbled on top of a sundae. And, of course, eating the cookie dough (preferably without raw eggs) is equally irresistible.

But the traditional recipe isn't enough for some. They make giant cookies or tiny ones, add more brown sugar and less granulated, and fold in candy and exotic nuts. Sometimes peanut butter, oatmeal, cocoa, or coconut is incorporated into the batter. Unexpected ingredients are added to the mix, such as pretzels, toffee, candied orange and lemon peel (or lime, clementine, or tangerine zest), zucchini, or even applesauce (not all in one cookie, one hopes). Sprinkling fancy sea salt on top of the unbaked cookie has become a standard practice in many bakeries. People even smash up different types of cookies to bake into their cookies.

Although chocolate chip cookies are delicious, as a dessert fanatic I was convinced that there were many more baked goods and other sweets that would benefit from dumping a bag of chips into their batter. To satisfy my curiosity, I consulted many of my pastry chef friends and bakers, and other assorted foodies. Their responses astonished me. Puddings, pies, ice cream, cakes, doughnuts, pastries, tarts, marshmallows, cocoa, bars, breads, and breakfast sweets were enthusiastically mentioned. The list was long and fabulous.

So, I decided to write *Chocolate Chip Sweets*, which goes far beyond the cookie. This collection of sweets for the home baker and professional is for all seasons and tastes. Many recipes are new takes on old-fashioned comfort desserts. Featured are signature recipes of world-class restaurants and boutique bakery shops, and personal and family treasures, all of which include this key ingredient— in chip, chunk, chopped, or coin form—as well as such add-ins as white or bittersweet chocolate, or enchanting chocolate crunchy pearls. There are not only classic recipes but also more inventive and challenging ones for the serious baker. Included are puddings and breads, honey cake, doughnuts, and even a rich Italian torta called *pinguino* (penguin cake), with Nutella and whipped cream and topped with a sprinkling of chocolate chips—a particular favorite from my childhood. Also included is a butter caramel sauce from Thomas Keller that pairs perfectly with a chocolate chip ice-cream sundae; homey oatmeal cookies, bursting with raisins and chocolate chips, from Lidia Bastianich; and Mario Batali's mother's simple-to-make chocolate chip banana bars, a favorite of his family.

There are still plenty of recipes to satisfy the chocolate chip cookie hound. I have been searching for a long time for the best cookie recipe—one with "real" chocolate chips, of course. Once I find that perfect recipe, it's on to the ultimate brownie or devil's food cake, studded with chips. These "best" recipes, along with many others, are not only in my go-to recipe box but are also featured on the following pages. They totally resonate with me—you will not find trendy concoctions made with foam infusions of olive oil, bacon, and hot chili peppers, flash frozen with dry ice, torched, and scorched, nor are preservatives or cheap chocolate used.

The featured recipes are certain to become part of your dessert repertoire. Whether served on a pretty silver tray or an elegant porcelain plate, or tucked into a lunch box, chocolate chip sweets are the perfect ending to a delightful meal or a satisfying snack. Your cookie jar, biscuit tin, or cake plate will quickly empty when filled with any of these delectable desserts.

BAKING WITH CHOCOLATE CHIPS

Most of these recipes—from chefs, pastry chefs, bakers, and restaurateurs—are quick and easy to prepare. Although I converted quantities in a number of the recipes from metric (more precise but less familiar to most home bakers) to standard American measurements, the proportions of the ingredients have remained the same. The recipes from restaurants have been reduced to small, manageable batches for the home baker. Each chef's voice has been retained as much as possible. You can learn a lot from these rock stars of the food world—the variations in their directions are like mini baking classes that provide a peek into their individual techniques. The recipe yields are approximate. If you use a level tablespoonful, there will be more, slightly smaller cookies than if a rounded tablespoonful is used.

The Kitchen: Essential Equipment and Tools

By starting with a clean, organized kitchen, you can probably do the dishes and put your pantry back in order before the timer dings and your goodies come out of the oven.

Stock your kitchen with the very best appliances and tools. Although you can mix your batter by hand, a KitchenAid stand mixer is a great investment. My lavender one is the workhorse (besides me) of my baking kitchen. You need only one, but invest in multiple work bowls, beaters, and whisks if you plan to do a lot of baking. The same goes for measuring cups, spoons, and silicone spatulas. For easy cookie forming, get three ice-cream scoops with spring-loaded handles—teaspoon, tablespoon, and cupcake sizes. You will also need a great rolling pin and some sturdy cookie cutters. Treat yourself to some basic baking pans, such as 8- or 9-inch round pans for layer cakes and a sturdy square baking pan, as well as pie pans and cupcake tins. Place a pile of half-sheet pans, about 13 by 18 inches (avoid the nonstick variety as their dark color will promote burned cookie bottoms) within reach, and have on hand a large quantity of parchment

paper sheets. Piping bags (if you choose the reusable ones, rinse in very hot water and never use detergent) and a variety of large tips are also handy, as are a bench scraper and an instant-read digital thermometer (and you will sometimes need deep-fry and candy thermometers, too). You can weigh out baking chocolate and chips on a digital scale. If your trash is many steps away, set out a large bowl or an empty, rinsed milk carton to act as your "pig." You have to dump it only once, after you finish baking.

The Well-Stocked Pantry

Stock your pantry with baking staples. These items include butter, flour, sugar, vanilla, chocolate, baking powder, and baking soda. Other ingredients are easily obtainable when needed. For example, unsweetened shredded coconut can be purchased in most health food stores. Always have unbleached all-purpose flour on hand. Be aware that some recipes direct you to use another type of flour, such as cake, pastry, bread, or whole wheat. Pure extracts, never artificial ones, are essential.

Choose the best-quality chocolate available. I always keep a three-kilo bag of Valrhona 70 percent dark chocolate pistoles (also called *fèves* or coins), and a variety of other chocolates in my freezer. Pistoles melt beautifully in a double boiler.

Chips come in many flavors and sizes. There are butterscotch, cappuccino, peanut butter, mint, and of course, many varieties of chocolate, such as bittersweet, semisweet, milk, and white. Consider using the amazing Valrhona pearls, perfect, tiny globes of chocolate or caramel, some with toasted cereal in the centers.

Make your own chocolate chips or chunks by chopping the pistoles by hand or in a food processor. This beats the dreaded, old-school method of hacking and sawing away at a block of chocolate. If you prefer to use chocolate chips rather than making your own, choose a high-quality brand of chips. Do not substitute chocolate chips when a recipe calls for melting baking chocolate, because the chips have substances added to keep them from completely melting.

Please use fresh, organic ingredients when possible; most everything else should also be unprocessed and chemical free. Shop at the farmers' market the day of or the day before baking. Purchase seasonal fruits. Dairy products, such as heavy cream, are certainly best right from the source. Unsalted butter is preferable for most recipes. Let the butter soften for a creamy batter. Make sure your baking essentials, such as jams, spices, and dried fruit (cherries, raisins, and berries), are also fresh. Nuts, in particular, can get rancid.

Recipe Instructions

Before you bake, study the recipe. Sometimes the instructions require the dough to rest in the refrigerator for several hours or overnight. Take this information into consideration if you intend to whip up a batch of cookies or a birthday cake right away. Follow instructions carefully. Preheat the oven and butter or line your pan with parchment paper, as directed.

A Few Basic Techniques

A practice I highly recommend is to prepare your baking setup by putting everything in place (this is known as *mise en place*) by measuring out each ingredient and laying out each piece of equipment needed. You will be able to tell right away if there is enough (or none) of a particular ingredient, or if it isn't fresh. Go to the store to fill in missing items before baking. The beauty of preparing your *mise en place* is that if you are interrupted during baking, you'll be able to continue without missing a beat. Upon returning to the kitchen from answering the door or phone (or anything else that calls you away), you'll know where you left off. Otherwise, you run the risk of adding twice as much of an ingredient, such as sugar—which most kids would say is a forgivable sin—or, heaven forbid, not adding any sugar at all. Make sure to sift flour (always spooned into a measuring cup, never scooped) and other dry ingredients into a bowl or onto a sheet of parchment paper and set aside until needed.

Master the basics of baking, and then experiment. Try substituting vanilla bean paste or the seeds scraped from a vanilla bean for pure vanilla extract, or an envelope of Italian leavening for baking soda or baking powder.

Large eggs are ideal—again, as fresh as possible. Crack each egg individually into a small, white ceramic bowl, and take a moment to look for bits of shells, which you will need to fish out. Discard an egg if there are blood spots and then start again with a clean bowl. Add one egg at a time to the batter, and then crack and check the next one. Stay safe—no tasting the batter, as consuming raw eggs can be dangerous to your health.

Enjoy baking like a skilled professional, and share your new favorite confections featuring chocolate chips with friends and family. Although I am a bit of a snob about fresh ingredients, I occasionally make junk food exceptions for crazy add-ins, like cereal, candy, marshmallows, and potato chips smooshed into the batter. I call these Kitchen Sink Cookies. Make an extra pie or batch of brownies, overflowing with chocolate chips, for someone homebound or for new parents—this gesture will bring great joy. Include the beautiful pan (and a copy of the recipe, too) as part of the gift. Sweets make people happy. Go in the kitchen and start baking.

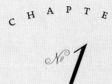

JACQUES TORRES CHOCOLATE CHIP COOKIES

Jacques Torres of Jacques Torres Chocolate

These amazing cookies from the famed chocolatier are filled with an astonishing amount of rich chocolate. You can customize this perennial picnic-basket favorite by adding dried fruit, nuts, chocolate chips, or candy bits. For ice-cream sandwiches, Chef Torres suggests filling them with homemade vanilla, coffee, raspberry, strawberry, peanut butter, or chocolate ice cream.

• MAKES ABOUT 18 LARGE COOKIES

2¼ cups plus 2 tablespoons all-purpose flour

1 teaspoon salt

¾ teaspoon baking powder

¾ teaspoon baking soda

6 ounces (1½ sticks) unsalted butter, softened

1 cup plus 2 tablespoons packed light brown sugar

¾ cup plus 1 tablespoon granulated sugar

1 large egg and 1 large egg yolk, at room temperature, lightly beaten

1 teaspoon pure vanilla extract

14 ounces (2⅓ cups) bittersweet chocolate, chopped into bite-size pieces

Preheat the oven to 325°F. Line two half-sheet pans with parchment paper, and set aside.

In a medium bowl, stir together the flour, salt, baking powder, and baking soda, and set aside.

In the bowl of a stand mixer fitted with the paddle attachment, beat the butter on medium speed for about 5 minutes, or until very light and fluffy. Add the brown sugar and granulated sugar, and beat until well blended.

Add the egg and egg yolk, and beat just until incorporated. Beat in the vanilla. Reduce the speed to low and add the flour mixture a little at a time, beating after each addition until incorporated. When all of the flour mixture has been incorporated, remove the bowl from the mixer and, using a silicone

spatula, fold in the chopped chocolate.

To shape the cookies, scoop out heaping tablespoonfuls of the dough and, with the palms of your hands, form them into 3-inch balls. Place the balls on the prepared pans, spacing them about 1 inch apart. Bake for about 15 minutes, or until lightly browned around the edges. Remove the cookies from the oven, transfer to wire racks, and let cool completely.

JUMBO CHOCOLATE CHIP COOKIES

Florian Bellanger of Mad Mac Macaron

Pastry chef Bellanger's cookies are meant to be huge and soft in the center. Knowing I adore these treats, he sent me a jumbo scoop as a birthday surprise— now I can make them anytime. · MAKES 16 EXTRA-LARGE COOKIES

3 cups sifted all-purpose flour

1 teaspoon baking soda

8 ounces (2 sticks) unsalted butter, softened

¾ cup granulated sugar

¾ cup packed light brown sugar

1 teaspoon pure vanilla extract

1 teaspoon sea salt

2 extra-large eggs

14 ounces (2⅓ cups) large bittersweet chocolate chips

1¾ cups crushed walnuts

In a medium bowl, stir together the flour and baking soda, and set aside.

In the bowl of a stand mixer fitted with the paddle attachment, beat the butter, granulated sugar, brown sugar, vanilla, and salt on medium speed until very light and fluffy. On low speed, add the eggs, one at a time. Add the dry ingredients just until incorporated. With a silicone spatula, fold in the chocolate chips and walnuts. Refrigerate the dough, covered with plastic wrap, for about 2 hours.

When you are ready to bake, preheat the oven to 350°F. Line two half-sheet pans with parchment paper.

Using a very large ice-cream scoop (3 inches in diameter), scoop out 16 cookies and place them on the prepared pans. Bake for about 21 minutes, or until lightly browned around the edges. Remove the cookies from the oven, transfer to wire racks, and let cool completely.

CHEF AQUINO'S CHOCOLATE CHIP COOKIES

Frederick Aquino of The Standard Grill, High Line

Chef Aquino's grandmother let him have warm cookies and milk before bed-time when he was a young boy. Bake his extraordinary cookies, based on this childhood memory, serve them with cream-top milk, and everyone will love you just a little bit more. · MAKES ABOUT 36 COOKIES

3 cups all-purpose flour

1 teaspoon baking soda

½ teaspoon salt

8 ounces (2 sticks) unsalted butter, softened

1 cup granulated sugar

1 cup packed light brown sugar

2 teaspoons pure vanilla extract

2 large eggs

12 ounces (2 cups) bittersweet or semisweet chocolate chips

Sea salt, for sprinkling

Preheat the oven to 375°F. Line three half-sheet pans with parchment paper, and set aside.

Into a medium bowl, sift the flour, baking soda, and salt, and set aside.

In the bowl of a stand mixer fitted with the paddle attachment, beat the butter, granulated sugar, brown sugar, and vanilla on medium speed until very light and fluffy. Add the eggs, one at a time. Add the dry ingredients and mix just until incorporated. With a silicone spatula, fold in the chocolate chips.

Drop rounded heaping tablespoonfuls of dough onto the prepared pans. Sprinkle sea salt on each cookie. Bake for 10 to 12 minutes, until golden. Remove the cookies from the oven, transfer to wire racks, and let cool completely.

MALTED CHOCOLATE CHIP COOKIES

Miro Uskokovic of Gramercy Tavern

Pastry chef Uskokovic often makes his exquisite chocolate chip cookies with crunchy pearls. But sometimes he will be inventive and add chopped-up malted milk balls instead. The type of malt powder called for in this recipe is used in bread and bagel baking. • MAKES ABOUT 24 COOKIES

¾ cup cake flour

1 cup bread flour

1 tablespoon non-diastatic malt powder

½ teaspoon baking soda

4 ounces (1 stick) unsalted butter, softened

1 teaspoon pure vanilla extract

½ cup granulated sugar

½ cup packed light brown sugar

Generous pinch of kosher salt

1 extra-large egg

3 ounces (½ cup) semisweet or bittersweet chocolate chips

1½ ounces (¼ cup) Valrhona crunchy pearls or chopped chocolate malted milk balls

Coarse sea salt, for sprinkling

Into a medium bowl, sift together the cake flour, bread flour, malt powder, and baking soda, and set aside.

In the bowl of a stand mixer fitted with the paddle attachment, cream the butter, vanilla, granulated sugar, brown sugar, and kosher salt until light and fluffy. Add the egg. Add the dry ingredients, and mix just until incorporated. With a silicone spatula, fold in the chocolate chips and crunchy pearls, and mix just until incorporated. Refrigerate the dough, covered with plastic wrap, for about 1 hour.

Preheat the oven to 350°F. Line two half-sheet pans with parchment paper.

Using a medium ice-cream scoop, scoop the dough and place the cookies on the prepared pans, spacing them 2 inches apart. Sprinkle each cookie with sea salt. Bake for 10 to 12 minutes if you prefer gooey centers, or up to 15 minutes for crispier edges. Remove the cookies from the oven, transfer to wire racks, and let cool for a few minutes. Serve warm with a glass of cold milk.

CHEF CONSIDINE'S CHOCOLATE CHIP COOKIES

Sean Considine of ABC Kitchen

Chef Considine's tempting, sweet cookies are jam-packed with melted chocolate chunks. Bring a tin of them to school or the office on an ordinary day, just to make everyone smile. · MAKES ABOUT 30 COOKIES

3¾ cups all-purpose flour

1 teaspoon baking soda

1 teaspoon salt

10 ounces (2½ sticks) unsalted butter, softened

1½ cups granulated sugar

⅔ cup packed light brown sugar

1 large egg, at room temperature

½ teaspoon pure vanilla extract

1 tablespoon honey

3 tablespoons crème fraîche

14 ounces (2⅓ cups) Valrhona Caraibe 66 percent chocolate, chopped or in small pieces

Preheat the oven to 350°F. Line three half-sheet pans with parchment paper, and set aside.

Into a medium bowl, sift the flour, baking soda, and salt, and set aside.

In the bowl of a stand mixer fitted with the paddle attachment, beat the butter, granulated sugar, and brown sugar on medium speed for about 5 minutes, or until very light and fluffy. Add the egg. Add the vanilla, honey, and crème fraîche. Add the dry ingredients and mix just until incorporated. With a silicone spatula, fold in the chopped chocolate.

Using a #30 scoop (about 2 tablespoons), place balls of dough onto the prepared pans. Bake for about 10 minutes, or until lightly browned around the edges. Remove from the oven, transfer to wire racks, and let cool completely.

ORANGE-RAISIN CHOCOLATE CHIP COOKIES

Tracey Zabar

When I was young, I had my first taste of raisin cookies in France. I was later amazed that a family friend, who once worked in a pâtisserie in Europe, was able to teach me how to make similar cookies. The recipe and some techniques have changed over the years—he made them in one big sheet, and when they cooled, just broke off pieces. I've modified his recipe by adding Italian baking powder, which makes the cookies extra sweet and delicate. • MAKES ABOUT 45 COOKIES

1½ cups all-purpose flour

½ cup almond flour

1 envelope Italian vanilla-scented baking powder

4 ounces (1 stick) unsalted butter, softened

½ cup granulated sugar

Grated zest of 1 orange

2 large eggs

½ cup raisins

3 ounces (½ cup) bittersweet or semisweet chocolate chips

Turbinado or coarse sugar, for sprinkling

In a medium bowl, combine the all-purpose flour, almond flour, and baking powder, and set aside.

In the bowl of a stand mixer fitted with the paddle attachment, cream the butter, granulated sugar, and orange zest. Add the eggs, one at a time. Add the dry ingredients, and mix just until combined. With a silicone spatula, fold in the raisins and chocolate chips.

On your work surface, lay out a piece of parchment paper that is the size of the bottom of a half-sheet pan, place the dough on top, and flatten it a bit. Add another piece of parchment on top, and roll out the dough with a rolling pin until it is about ½ inch thick. Place the 2 pieces of parchment with the dough inside in the refrigerator for about 30 minutes.

Preheat the oven to 350°F. Set aside two half-sheet pans.

Remove the dough from the refrigerator, peel off the top sheet of parchment, and place the parchment, sticky side up, on one of the pans. Cut out the cookies on the bottom piece of parchment with a square (or any desired shape) 1½-inch cookie cutter. Place half of the cookies on the prepared pan. Place the parchment with the remaining cookies on the second pan. Space the cookies evenly on the pans. Sprinkle the turbinado sugar on top of each cookie.

Bake for 11 to 13 minutes, until lightly browned on the edges. Remove the cookies from the oven, transfer to wire racks, and let cool completely.

NOTE: Instead of Italian baking powder (such as Lievito Pane degli Angeli), substitute 1½ teaspoons baking powder plus 1 teaspoon pure vanilla extract.

VARIATION: Substitute the grated zest of 2 lemons or tangerines for the orange zest.

CINNAMON CHOCOLATE CHIP SANDIES

Tracey Zabar

These teatime morsels, named after my favorite editor, are sweet, dotted with chocolate chips, and indeed quite sandy, with their surprising hint of cinnamon.

• MAKES ABOUT 20 TO 30 SMALL COOKIES

1¼ cups all-purpose flour
½ teaspoon salt
½ teaspoon ground cinnamon
4 ounces (1 stick) unsalted butter, softened
½ cup granulated sugar

1 large egg
1½ teaspoons pure vanilla extract
12 ounces (2 cups) bittersweet or semisweet chocolate chips
Coarse sugar, for sprinkling

Into a medium bowl, sift together the flour, salt, and cinnamon, and set aside.

In the bowl of a stand mixer fitted with the paddle attachment, cream the butter and granulated sugar. Add the egg and vanilla. Add the dry ingredients, just until incorporated. With a silicone spatula, fold in the chocolate chips.

Lay out a piece of parchment paper that is the size of the bottom of a half-sheet pan. Place the dough on top, and flatten the dough a bit. Add another piece of parchment on top, and roll out the dough, on top of the paper, with a rolling pin until the dough is about ½ inch thick. Place the 2 pieces of parchment, with the dough inside, in the refrigerator for about 30 minutes.

Preheat the oven to 350°F. Set aside two half-sheet pans.

Remove the dough from the refrigerator. Place the top sheet of parchment, sticky side up, on one of the pans. Cut out cookies with a heart-shape (or any desired shape) 1- or 2-inch cookie cutter.

Place half of the cookies on the prepared pan, and place the bottom parchment, with the remaining cookies, on the second pan. Space the cookies evenly on the pans. Sprinkle the coarse sugar on top of each cookie. Bake for 10 to 12 minutes, until lightly browned around the edges. Remove the cookies from the oven, transfer to wire racks, and let cool completely.

CHOCOLATE SHORTBREAD COOKIES

Anna Boisture of Le Pain Quotidien

Baker Boisture fell in love with Belgium's deep, dark, slightly bitter chocolate treats and developed this sublime cookie. She says, "My secret indulgence is to spread a bit of a favorite blue cheese, Valdeón, between two of these cookies, which will create a heavenly sweet-and-salty artisanal cookie sandwich. If you haven't tried chocolate and blue cheese together, you are missing out on one of the hidden gems of flavor pairings." · MAKES 24 COOKIES

1⅓ cups all-purpose flour

½ teaspoon salt

¼ cup dark or black cocoa powder

13 tablespoons unsalted butter, cold

1 cup confectioners' sugar

1 to 2 teaspoons water, as needed

1½ ounces (¼ cup) bittersweet chocolate chunks, roughly chopped

In a medium bowl, sift the flour, salt, and cocoa powder, and set aside.

Soften the butter by beating it with a rolling pin. You want it to be cold but malleable. By hand, using a bowl scraper, or in the bowl of a stand mixer fitted with the paddle attachment, cream together the butter and confectioners' sugar until light and fluffy. If using a mixer, be careful not to over-cream the mixture, as this will incorporate too much air. Add the flour mixture, and work it until the dough comes together. Add the water if the dough seems too dry. With a spatula, add the chocolate chunks, 1 tablespoon at a time.

Roll the dough into a log 2 inches in diameter, and then flatten each of the four sides to create a square log. Wrap in plastic wrap or parchment paper. Refrigerate the dough for at least 1 hour, or up to 3 days.

Preheat the oven to 325°F. Line a cookie sheet with parchment paper.

Using a sharp chef's knife, slice the dough into ¼-inch-thick cookies. Place the cookies on the prepared pan, at least 1 inch apart. Bake for about 15 minutes for a softer cookie, or up to 20 minutes for a crumbly cookie. The cookies will be quite soft when you remove them from the oven but will set as they cool. Cool completely on the pan.

GINGER-PECAN CHOCOLATE CHIP SHORTBREAD

Cara Tannenbaum of the Institute of Culinary Education

A traditional shortbread is crumbly and buttery, with a hint of vanilla flavoring. The recent trend is to add spices and other unconventional ingredients, such as chili peppers, into baked goods and confections. If you love the combination of ginger, chocolate, and nuts, you will adore Chef Tannenbaum's cookies.

• MAKES 12 COOKIES

¾ pound (3 sticks) unsalted butter, softened, plus more for the pan
1¼ cups confectioners' sugar
1 teaspoon pure vanilla extract
3 cups all-purpose flour
1 teaspoon ground ginger

½ teaspoon salt
½ cup candied ginger, diced small
4½ ounces (¾ cup) semisweet chocolate chips
½ cup coarsely chopped pecans

Preheat the oven to 325°F. Line a quarter-sheet pan with parchment paper, butter the paper and sides of the pan, and set aside.

In the bowl of a stand mixer fitted with the paddle attachment, beat the butter on medium speed for 1 minute. Add the confectioners' sugar, and beat until light and airy, about 3 minutes. Add the vanilla and mix.

Lower the speed of the mixer, and add the flour, ground ginger, and salt. Mix just until combined. Fold in the candied ginger, chocolate chips, and pecans.

Press the dough evenly into the prepared pan. Bake for 20 to 25 minutes, until set and lightly golden. Remove the shortbread from the oven, cool completely in the pan, then cut into 12 rectangles.

CHOCOLATE BISCOTTI

Tracey Zabar

In Italy, all cookies are called biscotti. If there are olive trees in the town, olive oil is used in the recipes. If you look out the window and there are cows grazing, chances are that butter will be substituted for the olive oil. I once taught an Italian pastry chef to bake my version of buttery biscotti in his kitchen, located in a town where olive oil is king. He loved them so much that, to my delight, he has added Biscotti Tracey Zabar to his restaurant menu. These biscotti are softer than the traditional ones served in America. Enjoy them dunked in milk, coffee, or wine. • MAKES ABOUT 45 COOKIES

2 cups all-purpose flour

2 teaspoons instant espresso powder

2 teaspoons baking powder

½ teaspoon salt

½ cup Dutch-process cocoa powder

4 ounces (1 stick) unsalted butter, softened

1 cup granulated sugar

2 large eggs

2 teaspoons pure vanilla extract

Grated zest of 1 orange

3 ounces (½ cup) bittersweet or semisweet chocolate chips

3 ounces (½ cup) Valrhona crunchy pearls

½ cup sanding (coarse) sugar, divided

Preheat the oven to 350°F. Line two half-sheet pans with parchment paper, and set aside.

In a medium bowl, whisk together the flour, espresso powder, baking powder, and salt. Sift in the cocoa, whisk to combine, and set aside.

In the bowl of a stand mixer fitted with the paddle attachment, cream the butter and granulated sugar. Add the eggs, vanilla, and orange zest. Add the dry ingredients, and mix just until combined. With a wooden spoon, fold in the chocolate chips and crunchy pearls.

Sprinkle ¼ cup of the sanding sugar on the parchment in each prepared pan. Divide the dough into 4 pieces. Roll out each piece into a log about 12 inches long and 2 inches in diameter. The dough will be somewhat sticky. Place 2 logs on each of the pans, and roll the logs in the sanding sugar until most of it coats the logs.

Bake for 25 to 30 minutes, making sure the logs do not start to burn. Remove the pans from the oven, and leave the oven turned on. Cool the logs for about 10 minutes, then cut diagonally into 1-inch pieces. (It is perfectly acceptable if the logs have some cracks on the top or crumble a bit under the knife blade.) Lay the cookies, flat side down, on the pans and return the pans to the oven for 5 minutes. Remove from the oven, flip the cookies over, and return to the oven for another 5 minutes to dry out. Remove the cookies from the oven, transfer to wire racks, and let cool completely.

HONEY CHOCOLATE CHIP COOKIES

Mina Pizarro of Juni

Pastry chef Pizarro's cookies are chewy and oozing with honey. The first time I ate one, it was paired with Mint Chocolate Chip Ice Cream (page 137), a combination that is seductive. • MAKES 12 LARGE COOKIES

1 cup all-purpose flour
1½ teaspoons baking powder
1 teaspoon baking soda
⅓ cup (5⅓ tablespoons) unsalted
   butter, softened

4 teaspoons granulated sugar
⅓ cup packed dark brown sugar
½ cup honey
4½ ounces (¾ cup) bittersweet
   chocolate, coarsely chopped

Preheat the oven to 350°F. Line two half-sheet pans with parchment paper, and set aside.

Into a medium bowl, sift together the flour, baking powder, and baking soda, and set aside.

In the bowl of a stand mixer fitted with the paddle attachment, cream the butter, granulated sugar, brown sugar, and honey. Add the dry ingredients, and mix just until combined. Fold in the chopped chocolate.

Scoop out about 2 rounded tablespoons of the dough for each cookie, and place 6 cookies on each of the prepared pans. Gently push down on each cookie to flatten slightly. Bake for 12 to 15 minutes, until golden brown. Remove the cookies from the oven, transfer to wire racks, and let cool completely.

SALTED PISTACHIO, CHERRY, AND WHITE CHOCOLATE CHIP COOKIES

Carolynn Spence of Chateau Marmont

Chef Spence's cookies are beautifully speckled with white chips, pistachios, and dried cherries. These chewy, salty wonders will become a cookie jar favorite in your kitchen. • MAKES ABOUT 30 COOKIES

1 cup dried sour cherries

1 ounce amaretto liqueur

¾ cup water

2½ cups all-purpose flour

1 teaspoon baking soda

½ teaspoon kosher salt

8 ounces (2 sticks) unsalted butter, softened

¼ cup pistachio paste

Seeds scraped from ½ vanilla bean

¾ cup granulated sugar

1 cup packed dark brown sugar

3 large eggs, at room temperature

1 teaspoon pure almond extract

6 ounces (1 cup) white chocolate chips

1 cup shelled pistachios, roughly chopped in a food processor fitted with the metal blade

1 tablespoon Maldon sea salt

In a small bowl, soak the cherries in amaretto and water, and set aside.

Into a medium bowl, sift flour, baking soda, and kosher salt, and set aside.

In the bowl of a stand mixer fitted with the paddle attachment, cream the butter. Add the pistachio paste and vanilla seeds. Add the granulated sugar and brown sugar, and mix until creamy. Add the eggs, one at a time, and then add the almond extract. Add the dry ingredients, and mix just until incorporated.

Drain the cherries, and fold them into the batter. Add the white chocolate chips, chopped pistachios, and sea salt. Place the bowl, covered with plastic wrap, in the refrigerator for 1 hour.

Preheat the oven to 375°F. Line two half-sheet pans with parchment paper.

Scoop tablespoon-size balls of dough onto the prepared pans. Bake for 8 to 10 minutes, or until golden brown. Remove the cookies from the oven, transfer to wire racks, and let cool completely.

CRANBERRY-ORANGE CHOCOLATE CHIP OATMEAL COOKIES

Alexandra Prats of Michael's

Pastry chef Prats loves these cookies, studded with cranberries, orange, and bittersweet chocolate, for the holidays. You can also use any combination of other dried fruits and types of chocolate chips. · MAKES ABOUT 30 COOKIES

1½ cups all-purpose flour

2⅔ cups old-fashioned rolled oats

1 teaspoon baking soda

1 teaspoon salt

¾ teaspoon ground allspice

8 ounces (2 sticks) unsalted butter, softened

¾ cup granulated sugar

1 cup packed light brown sugar

2 large eggs

1 teaspoon orange liqueur, such as Grand Marnier

Grated zest of 1 orange

¾ cup dried cranberries

6 ounces (1 cup) bittersweet chocolate chips

In a medium bowl, whisk together the flour, oats, baking soda, salt, and allspice, and set aside.

In the bowl of a stand mixer fitted with the paddle attachment, cream together the butter, granulated sugar, and brown sugar on medium speed until light and fluffy. Add the eggs and liqueur. Add the orange zest.

On low speed, add the dry ingredients just until combined. Add the cranberries and chocolate chips just until combined. Chill the dough, covered with plastic wrap, in the refrigerator for 1 hour.

Preheat the oven to 350°F. Line three half-sheet pans with parchment paper.

Scoop out about 2 rounded tablespoonfuls of the dough onto the prepared pans, spacing the cookies 1 inch apart. Press your thumb into the center of each cookie to flatten. Bake for 7 to 10 minutes, rotating the pans halfway through, until the cookies have browned edges. The centers will look slightly undercooked. They will continue baking as they cool. Remove the cookies from the oven, transfer to wire racks, and let cool completely.

OATMEAL RAISIN COOKIES WITH CHOCOLATE CHIPS

Lidia Bastianich of Lidia's Italy

Every year at Christmastime Chef Bastianich's daughter, Tanya, invites me to Lidia's restaurant, Felidia, for lunch. The two of us catch up on our families and share my favorite dish, pasta Bolognese. For dessert, I am always presented with my very own cookie plate. This cookie, Lidia's own, is one of the stars of that assortment. • MAKES ABOUT 54 COOKIES

2½ cups all-purpose flour

2 cups quick-cooking oats (not instant)

1½ teaspoons baking soda

1 teaspoon salt

8 ounces (2 sticks) unsalted butter, melted and cooled slightly

1½ cups packed light brown sugar

1 cup granulated sugar

3 large eggs, lightly beaten

1½ teaspoons pure vanilla extract

12 ounces (2 cups) semisweet chocolate chips

½ cup raisins

In a medium bowl, whisk the flour, oats, baking soda, and salt, and set aside.

In the bowl of a stand mixer fitted with the paddle attachment, beat the butter, brown sugar, and granulated sugar at high speed until pale and fluffy, 2 to 3 minutes. Add the eggs and beat until creamy, about 1 minute. Beat in the vanilla. Reduce the speed to low and mix in the dry ingredients just until combined, and then fold in the chocolate chips and raisins with a wooden spoon. Cover the dough with plastic wrap, and refrigerate for 30 minutes, or up to an hour.

Arrange racks in the top and bottom thirds of the oven. Preheat the oven to 350°F. Line two half-sheet pans with parchment paper.

Scoop the dough in 2 tablespoon–size portions and roll into balls. Arrange the balls 2 to 3 inches apart on the prepared pans. Bake for 14 to 15 minutes, until golden, rotating the pans halfway through baking. Remove the cookies from the oven, transfer to wire racks, and let cool completely.

PEANUT BUTTER CHOCOLATE CHIP COOKIES

Marc Murphy and Campbell Murphy of Landmarc

When I asked Chef Murphy for a recipe for peanut butter cookies with chocolate chips, he and his daughter, age eleven, came up with this gem—a sweet combination of peanut butter and chocolate. · MAKES ABOUT 40 COOKIES

4 ounces (1 stick) unsalted butter, softened, plus more for the pans
1 cup all-purpose flour
1 cup old-fashioned rolled oats
½ teaspoon baking powder
½ teaspoon baking soda
½ teaspoon salt
½ cup granulated sugar

½ cup packed light brown sugar
1 large egg
½ teaspoon pure vanilla extract
3 tablespoons smooth or chunky peanut butter
6 ounces (1 cup) bittersweet or semisweet chocolate chips

Preheat the oven to 350°F. Butter two half-sheet pans, and set aside.

In a medium bowl, stir together the flour, oats, baking powder, baking soda, and salt, and set aside.

In the bowl of a stand mixer fitted with the paddle attachment, cream the butter, granulated sugar, and brown sugar. Blend in the egg, vanilla, and peanut butter. Add the dry ingredients, and mix until well blended. With a silicone spatula, fold in the chocolate chips.

Roll the dough into tablespoon-size balls, and place on the prepared pans. Bake for 12 minutes, or until lightly golden brown. Remove the cookies from the oven, transfer to a wire rack, and let cool completely.

PEANUT BUTTER—OATMEAL CHOCOLATE CHIP COOKIES

Karen DeMasco

Pastry chef DeMasco's hybrid of classic peanut butter, oatmeal, and chocolate chip cookies is her family's favorite. The salty pretzels and peanut butter balance wonderfully with the sugars and chocolate. They're oh so good.

• MAKES ABOUT 36 COOKIES

1½ cups all-purpose flour

1 cup quick-cooking oats (not instant)

2 teaspoons baking soda

½ teaspoon kosher salt

8 ounces (2 sticks) unsalted butter, softened

½ cup packed dark brown sugar

½ cup granulated sugar

1 teaspoon pure vanilla extract

2 large eggs

¾ cup smooth peanut butter

12 ounces (2 cups) mini chocolate chips

3 ounces (1½ cups) crushed pretzel pieces

Preheat the oven to 350°F. Line two half-sheet pans with parchment paper, and set aside.

In a medium bowl, combine the flour, oats, baking soda, and salt; set aside.

In the bowl of a stand mixer fitted with the paddle attachment, combine the butter, brown sugar, granulated sugar, and vanilla on medium speed. Scrape down the sides of the bowl. Add the eggs, one at a time. Add the peanut butter. Add the dry ingredients in three additions, and combine each one completely before adding the next. With a silicone spatula, gently fold in the chocolate chips and pretzels.

Spoon tablespoon-size balls of dough onto the prepared pans, allowing 1 inch of space between each cookie. Using your fingers or the bottom of a measuring cup, tap down each cookie to form a disk. Bake for 8 to 10 minutes, rotating the pan 180 degrees halfway through. Look for a risen cookie that is golden around the edges and still soft in the center. Remove the cookies from the oven, and let cool completely on the pans.

CHAPTER

№ 2

PARTY

COOKIES

CHOCOLATE COOKIES

Dominique Ansel of Dominique Ansel Bakery

I had the nerve to ask my friend pastry chef Ansel to mess with his perfect cookie recipe. He graciously allowed me to make these rich cookies without pecans to satisfy those who don't care for nuts. • MAKES ABOUT 18 LARGE COOKIES

11 ounces 66 percent chocolate,
   preferably Valrhona Caraibe
3 tablespoons unsalted butter
3 large eggs
1 cup plus 1 teaspoon granulated sugar

½ cup all-purpose flour
1 teaspoon baking powder
1 teaspoon salt
3 ounces (½ cup) 70 percent chocolate
   chips, preferably Valrhona Guanaja

Preheat the oven to 325°F. Line two half-sheet pans with parchment paper, and set aside.

In the top of a double boiler over low heat, melt the 66 percent chocolate and butter. Remove from the heat and set aside to cool for a few minutes.

In the bowl of a stand mixer fitted with the paddle attachment, beat the eggs and sugar. Add the melted chocolate mixture, then the flour, baking powder, and salt, and mix just until combined. Remove the bowl from the mixer, and fold in the chocolate chips.

Shape the dough into balls the size of golf balls, and arrange them on the prepared pans. Bake for 8 to 10 minutes. The edges will feel done, but the centers will feel slightly underdone. Remove the cookies from the oven, transfer to wire racks, and let cool completely.

TRIPLE CHOCOLATE MADNESS COOKIES

Nicole Kaplan of Rôtisserie Georgette

Pastry chef Kaplan's mouth-watering cookies are a chocolate lover's delight. They disappear in my house before they cool off. · MAKES ABOUT 40 COOKIES

½ cup cake flour

2 tablespoons Dutch-process cocoa powder, sifted

¼ teaspoon baking powder

Pinch of salt

3 ounces (¾ stick) unsalted butter

4 ounces unsweetened chocolate

6 ounces semisweet chocolate

3 large eggs

1 cup granulated sugar

6 ounces (1 cup) mixed (milk, semisweet, and white) chocolate chunks

Fleur de sel, for sprinkling

Preheat the oven to 325°F. Line two half-sheet pans with parchment paper, and set aside.

In a medium bowl, stir together the cake flour, cocoa powder, baking powder, and salt, and set aside.

In the top of a double boiler, over medium heat, melt the butter, unsweetened chocolate, and semisweet chocolate, and set aside to cool for about 5 minutes.

In the bowl of a stand mixer fitted with the paddle attachment, ribbon together the eggs and sugar. Add the melted chocolate mixture to the egg mixture. Stir in the dry ingredients. Add the chocolate chunks. Let rest for a few minutes to firm up.

Scoop the batter into walnut-size balls, and place evenly on the prepared pans. Bake for about 5 minutes, allowing the center of each cookie to remain slightly soft. Remove the cookies from the oven, immediately sprinkle each cookie with fleur de sel, transfer to wire racks, and let cool completely.

CHOCOLATE CHUBBIES

Sarabeth Levine of Sarabeth's Bakery

I have been the proud owner of this quintessential recipe for twenty-five years. Thank you, Sarabeth, my baking friend. For this book, I asked her to make her cookies without nuts, the way I do. Here is the marvelous result.

• MAKES ABOUT 24 COOKIES

½ cup all-purpose flour

½ teaspoon baking powder

¼ teaspoon salt

4 ounces (1 stick) unsalted butter, cut into ½-inch cubes

8 ounces (1⅓ cups) bittersweet or semisweet (no more than 62 percent cacao) chocolate, finely chopped

3 ounces (½ cup) unsweetened chocolate, finely chopped

3 large eggs, at room temperature

1¼ cups granulated sugar

2 teaspoons pure vanilla extract

12 ounces (2 cups) bittersweet or semisweet chocolate chips

Preheat the oven to 350°F. Line three half-sheet pans with parchment paper, and set aside.

Into a medium bowl, sift together the flour, baking powder, and salt, and set aside.

In the top of a double boiler, over medium heat, melt the butter, bittersweet chocolate, and unsweetened chocolate. Set aside to cool for about 5 minutes.

In the bowl of a stand mixer fitted with the whip attachment, beat the eggs until foamy and thickened. Gradually add the sugar, and beat until a thick ribbon forms. Add the vanilla, and whip until the eggs are very pale, about 3 minutes. Beat in the melted chocolate mixture. Add the dry ingredients, and mix just until combined. Using a silicone spatula, fold in the chocolate chips.

Using a 2-inch ice-cream scoop, drop the cookies onto the prepared pans. Bake for 17 to 20 minutes, until set around the edges. Remove the cookies from the oven, and let cool completely on the pans.

HAZELNUT CRACKLES

Tracey Zabar

These chocolate cookies were a staple at bakeries in my hometown. An old Italian friend shared this recipe for my favorite crackles, with the addition of chocolate chips, of course. · MAKES ABOUT 18 COOKIES

1¼ cups granulated sugar, divided
1 cup confectioners' sugar, for rolling
1 tablespoon unsalted butter, cut into
  ½-inch cubes
6 ounces (1 cup) bittersweet
  chocolate, chopped
1 large egg

½ teaspoon baking powder
½ cup hazelnut flour
¼ cup all-purpose flour
½ teaspoon salt
1½ ounces (¼ cup) bittersweet or
  semisweet chocolate chips

Preheat the oven to 325°F. Line two half-sheet pans with parchment paper, and set aside.

Place 1 cup of the granulated sugar in a shallow bowl, and the confectioners' sugar in a second shallow bowl, and set aside.

In the top of a double boiler, over medium heat, melt the butter and bittersweet chocolate, and set aside to cool for a few minutes.

In the bowl of a stand mixer fitted with the paddle attachment, beat the egg and the remaining ¼ cup granulated sugar until thick, about 5 minutes. Add the melted chocolate mixture and mix. Add the baking powder, hazelnut flour, all-purpose flour, and salt, and mix, just until incorporated. With a silicone spatula, fold in the chocolate chips.

Scoop the batter into walnut-size balls, and roll them in the reserved granulated sugar, then in the confectioners' sugar, coating them generously. Place the cookies on the prepared pans. Bake for 11 to 13 minutes. The cookies will have a cracked appearance. Remove the cookies from the oven, transfer to wire racks, and let cool completely.

SALTED CHOCOLATE CHIP AND PECAN MERINGUE BITES

Amanda Cook of Tenth Avenue Cookshop

Every Christmas during her childhood, pastry chef Cook and her family spent many hours baking. This dessert was traditionally made at the end of the day. The family called these the Nighty-Night Cookies because when they put them in the oven they would say, "Good night," and by some baking miracle, the oven would be filled with wonderful cookies the next morning. She did not realize that the cookies were simply meringues, which dried out overnight. Her childhood favorite, these magical cookies now have the added touches of pecans and a pinch of salt to balance the sweet and make them more grown-up.

• MAKES ABOUT 40 COOKIES

3 large egg whites

1 cup granulated sugar

1 teaspoon pure vanilla extract

¾ teaspoon fine salt

¾ cup toasted pecans, finely chopped

4½ ounces (¾ cup) bittersweet or
    semisweet chocolate chips

Maldon sea salt, for sprinkling

Preheat the oven to 350°F. Line two half-sheet pans with parchment paper, and set aside.

In the bowl of a stand mixer fitted with the whip attachment, whisk the egg whites. Once they have became thick, white, and opaque, slowly add the sugar, about 2 tablespoons at a time, until the meringue is shiny and stiff peaks have formed. Add the vanilla, and then the fine salt. Remove the bowl from the mixer, then, using a silicone spatula, gently fold in the chopped pecans and chocolate chips.

Portion with a small spring-loaded ice-cream scoop onto the prepared pans. Top each one with a small pinch of Maldon salt. Place the pans in the oven, and immediately turn off the heat. Leave the pans in the oven, without opening the door, for at least 8 hours, or overnight.

CONGO BARS

Tracey Zabar

My congo bars consist of a chocolaty cake blanketed with a sensational topping. In the summer I like to place them, completely cooled, in the refrigerator for a while before cutting and serving. • MAKES 12 BARS

4 ounces (1 stick) unsalted butter, cut into 1-inch cubes, plus more for the pan

3 ounces (½ cup) unsweetened chocolate, coarsely chopped

2 large eggs

1 cup granulated sugar

½ teaspoon salt

1 cup all-purpose flour

½ cup unsweetened shredded coconut (optional)

6 ounces (1 cup) bittersweet or semisweet chocolate chips

½ cup mini marshmallows

½ cup coarsely chopped pecans or walnuts

Preheat the oven to 350°F. Butter a 4 by 13–inch tart pan with a removable bottom, and set aside.

In the top of a double boiler, over medium heat, melt the butter and unsweetened chocolate. Set aside for 5 minutes to cool.

In the bowl of a stand mixer fitted with the paddle attachment, beat the eggs and sugar for 5 minutes. Add the melted chocolate mixture. Add the salt and flour. Pour the batter into the prepared pan. Sprinkle the coconut (if using), then the chocolate chips, and finally the marshmallows and nuts on top.

Bake for about 30 minutes, or until the marshmallows and coconut (if using) just start to brown. Remove the cake from the oven, and let cool completely in the pan. Cover with plastic wrap, and place in the refrigerator for 1 hour. Remove from the pan, and cut into 12 bars.

VARIATION: S'MORE BARS

Replace the bittersweet or semisweet chocolate chips with milk chocolate chips. Omit the nuts. Replace the coconut with ½ cup crushed graham crackers.

COCONUT BARS

Nick Malgieri of the Institute of Culinary Education

Each fall a group of my pastry chef friends comes to my house for lunch. Nick's dessert contribution of coconut bars made me extra happy because his topping has a heaping amount of chocolate chips. · MAKES 24 BARS

CRUST

1½ cups all-purpose flour

3 tablespoons Dutch-process cocoa
    powder

½ teaspoon baking powder

¼ teaspoon salt

6 ounces (1½ sticks) unsalted butter,
    softened

½ cup granulated sugar

Set the oven rack in the lowest position. Preheat the oven to 350°F. Line a quarter-sheet pan with a large piece of parchment paper that extends beyond the rim of the pan by a few inches on each side. Butter the parchment.

Into a medium bowl, sift together the flour, cocoa powder, baking powder, and salt, and set aside.

In the bowl of a stand mixer fitted with the paddle attachment, cream the butter and granulated sugar on medium speed until light, 2 to 3 minutes. On low speed, add the flour mixture, and mix just until incorporated.

Place the dough in the prepared pan, and gently pat it into place with your hands. Bake for about 15 minutes, or until puffy in the center. Remove the crust from the oven, and leave the oven turned on.

⅔ cup granulated sugar

1¼ cups packed light brown sugar

2 teaspoons pure vanilla extract

4 large eggs

2⅔ cups unsweetened shredded coconut

8 ounces (2 cups) pecan halves

12 ounces (2 cups) bittersweet chocolate chips

In a large bowl, combine the granulated sugar, brown sugar, and vanilla. With a silicone spatula, mix the eggs, one at a time, into the sugar mixture, and stir until combined. Fold in the coconut, pecans, and chocolate chips. Spread this mixture on top of the baked crust.

Bake for 25 to 30 minutes, until golden brown and set. Remove the cake from the oven, and let cool for 15 minutes in the pan. Lift the cake out of the pan by the parchment edges, and place on a cutting board. Let cool completely before cutting into bars that are approximately 3 by 4 inches.

CHOCOLATE CHIP ROCHER

Daniel Boulud of Daniel

Chef Boulud told me, "*Rocher* is one of my favorite coconut preparations. To me, this cookie is a welcome change from the average selection of butter- and flour-laden, crumbly cookies available in the market. I like the not-too-sweet flavor and chewy texture. It also is very easy and fun to make, with only about a half hour of active assembly and baking time. Our customers love chocolate, so we enrich the preparation with chocolate chips inside the batter as well as in the outer glaze." • MAKES ABOUT 50 COOKIES

1¼ cups granulated sugar

4 large egg whites

½ cup corn syrup

3½ cups unsweetened extra-fine-shredded coconut

14 ounces (2⅓ cups) dark chocolate chips, divided

2 tablespoons grapeseed or canola oil

Preheat the oven to 375°F. Line two half-sheet pans with parchment paper, and set aside.

In a small heat-proof bowl, combine the sugar, egg whites, and corn syrup. Set the bowl over a pan of simmering water, creating a double boiler, and warm, stirring until the mixture reaches 120°F. Remove the pan from the heat and fold in the coconut. Allow the mixture to cool, and then fold in 1 cup of the chocolate chips.

Scoop chestnut-size spoonfuls of the batter and roll them between the palms of your hands to make balls (if your hands get sticky, wet them with cold water). Place the balls on the prepared sheets, approximately 1 inch apart.

Bake for 3 minutes, rotate the pans 180 degrees, and bake for another 2 minutes, or until golden brown. Remove the cookies from the oven, transfer to wire racks, and let cool completely.

In a medium heat-proof bowl, combine the remaining 1⅓ cups chocolate chips and the oil, and set over a pan of simmering water. Heat, stirring

occasionally, until melted. Remove from the heat, and stir with a silicone spatula until the chocolate cools to 95°F, measured on an instant-read thermometer. Dip the *rocher* cookies in the chocolate to cover halfway, and return them to the sheet pan. Chill in the refrigerator until the chocolate is set.

JAN HAGELS

Matthew Neele of Wallsé

This recipe for *jan hagels*, a traditional Dutch holiday treat, is from pastry chef Neele's grandmother, who lives in the Netherlands and is an amazing cook. He loved visiting the local markets with her as a child and learned from her how to combine spices for these extraordinary bar cookies. • MAKES 24 BARS

6 ounces (1½ sticks) unsalted butter, softened

½ cup granulated sugar

½ teaspoon ground cinnamon

½ teaspoon ground cloves

½ teaspoon ground allspice

2 cups minus 2 tablespoons all-purpose flour

¾ teaspoon baking powder

¼ teaspoon salt

2 tablespoons milk

¼ cup pearl sugar

1½ ounces (¼ cup) bittersweet chocolate, chopped, or bittersweet chocolate chips

Preheat the oven to 325°F. Line a half-sheet pan with parchment paper; set aside.

In the bowl of a stand mixer fitted with the paddle attachment, cream the butter, granulated sugar, cinnamon, cloves, and allspice until fluffy. Sift in the flour, baking powder, and salt, and mix just until combined. On a lightly floured surface, use a rolling pin to roll out the dough until it is approximately the size of the half-sheet pan. Place the dough in the prepared pan. Drizzle the milk onto the surface of the dough, and spread with your fingers. Sprinkle the pearl sugar and chopped chocolate evenly over the top.

Bake for about 15 minutes, or until the edges start to brown. Remove the bars from the oven, and cut into 2 by 3–inch bar cookies. Let cool completely.

NOTE: Instead of sprinkling the chopped chocolate over the top of the dough, drizzle chocolate melted (or tempered) in a double boiler over the top of the completely cooled bars.

PEANUT BUTTER CHOCOLATE CHIP BROWNIES

Elisa Strauss of Confetti Cakes

Pastry chef Strauss has a weakness for these brownies, which she serves with a glass of cold milk. Use chunky or smooth peanut butter; just don't turn to natural, as the oil separates. Whether enjoyed as an after-school snack or the ending to a meal, these brownies are a crowd pleaser. · MAKES 54 SMALL BROWNIES

1 pound (4 sticks) unsalted butter, plus extra, melted, for the pan

2 cups all-purpose flour

12 ounces (2 cups) bittersweet chocolate, chopped

6 large eggs

½ teaspoon salt

2 cups granulated sugar

2 cups packed dark brown sugar

1 tablespoon pure vanilla extract

9 ounces (1½ cups) semisweet chocolate chips

1 cup smooth or chunky peanut butter

Preheat the oven to 350°F. Line the bottom of a half-sheet pan with parchment paper. Brush the parchment and the sides of the pan with melted butter.

Into a large bowl, sift the flour, and set aside.

In the top of a double boiler over medium heat, melt 1 pound of the butter and bittersweet chocolate, and set aside to cool for a few minutes.

In the bowl of a stand mixer fitted with the paddle attachment, beat the eggs, salt, granulated sugar, brown sugar, and vanilla, and beat on low speed until combined. Slowly add the melted chocolate mixture, and beat on low speed until combined. Gently fold in the flour by hand, using a silicone spatula. Gently fold in the chocolate chips.

Pour the batter into the prepared pan and dollop the peanut butter on top. Use a butter knife to swirl the peanut butter through the batter to create a marbled look. Bang the pan against the table a few times to remove any air bubbles.

Bake for about 30 minutes, or until the top has formed a shiny crust and is moderately firm. Remove the brownies from the oven. Cool in the pan for

20 minutes, then release the brownies from the pan by running a metal spatula or knife along the sides. Flip the brownies over onto another pan or cake board and peel away the parchment. Flip again, so that the top side is up, and cut into 2-inch squares.

CHOCOLATE CHIP BLONDIES

Tracey Zabar

With its distinct butterscotch-brown sugar-caramel flavor, a blondie is a beloved cousin of the venerable brownie. The batter can be whipped up in minutes. These blondies can be transported easily, making them perfect for bake sales.

• MAKES 16 SQUARES

8 ounces (2 sticks) unsalted butter

2 cups packed light brown sugar

2 large eggs

1 tablespoon pure vanilla extract

2 cups all-purpose flour

2 teaspoons baking powder

½ teaspoon salt

6 ounces (1 cup) bittersweet chocolate chips

6 ounces (1 cup) Valrhona crunchy pearls

Preheat the oven to 350°F. Line an 8-inch square baking pan with parchment paper, and set aside.

In a small saucepan, melt the butter. Place the sugar in the heat-proof bowl of a stand mixer fitted with the paddle attachment. Pour the hot butter over the sugar, and mix. Add the eggs and vanilla, and mix. Add the flour, baking powder, and salt, and mix just until combined. With a silicone spatula, fold in the chocolate chips and crunchy pearls.

Spread the batter evenly in the prepared pan and smooth the top. Bake for about 45 minutes, or until the edges start to brown. Remove the blondies from the oven. Cool completely in the pan. Remove the blondies from the pan, wrap in plastic wrap, and place in the refrigerator for about 30 minutes. Cut into 2-inch squares.

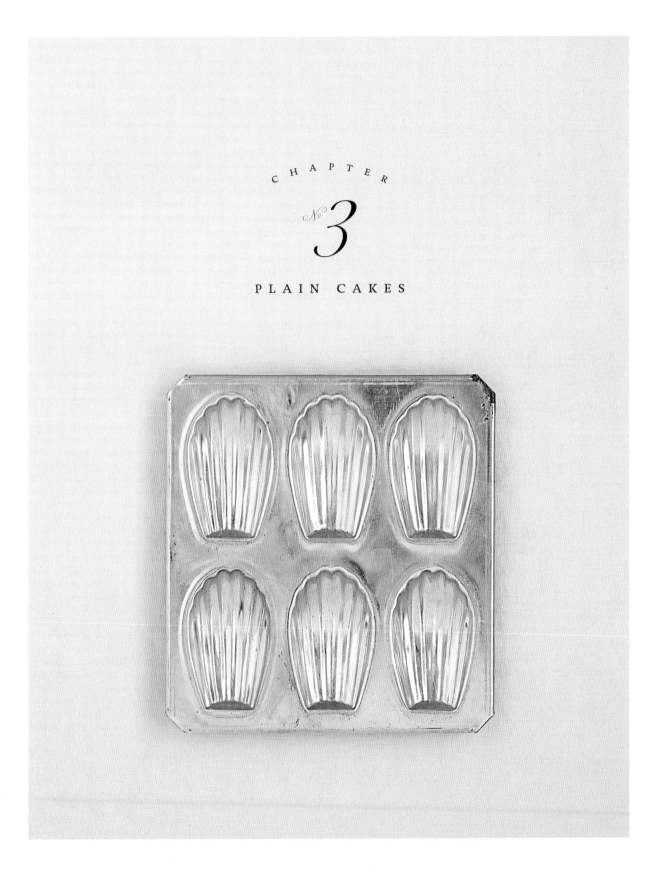

FRUIT CHOCOLATE CHIP TEA CAKE

Tracey Zabar

This simple cake is beloved in my house. The cherry chocolate chip version has been a perennial best seller at my sons' school bake sales. Buttery, sweet, and packed with fruit and chocolate, what's not to love? • MAKES 2 LOAVES

8 ounces (2 sticks) unsalted butter, softened, plus more for the pans

1½ cups granulated sugar, plus more for sugaring the pans

½ teaspoon salt

4 extra-large eggs, at room temperature

1 tablespoon pure vanilla extract

2 cups all-purpose flour

2 Anjou or Bosc pears, peeled, cored, and cubed

¼ cup raspberries

3 ounces (½ cup) bittersweet chocolate chips

3 ounces (½ cup) Valrhona crunchy pearls

Preheat the oven to 350°F. Generously butter two 8 by 5–inch loaf pans, and sprinkle a few teaspoons of sugar in each. Swirl the sugar around so that it coats the inside of the pans, and tap the excess out and discard. Set aside.

In the bowl of a stand mixer fitted with the paddle attachment, cream the butter, the remaining 1½ cups sugar, and the salt. Add the eggs, one at a time. Add the vanilla. Fold in the flour, just until incorporated. With a silicone spatula, gently fold in the pears, raspberries, chocolate chips, and crunchy pearls.

Pour the batter into the prepared pans. Bake for about 1 hour, or until golden brown and baked in the center. Remove the loaves from the oven, and cool in the pans for about 20 minutes. Remove the cakes from the pans, transfer to a wire rack, and let cool completely.

VARIATIONS: JAM SWIRL CHOCOLATE CHIP TEA CAKE
Omit the crunchy pearls. Pour one-quarter of the batter into each pan. Dollop ⅓ cup of jam, such as raspberry, strawberry, or orange marmalade, on top. Add the remaining batter and run a butter knife gently through the batter to swirl.

MIXED FRUIT CHOCOLATE CHIP TEA CAKE

Replace the pears and raspberries with ½ cup dried fruit, such as blueberries, cherries, or raisins; or with fresh fruit, such as apples (peeled, cored, and cubed), figs (stems removed and chopped), or berries.

Optional: Using a Microplane, zest ½ orange, 1 lemon, 1 tangerine, or 1 lime. Add the zest when creaming the butter and sugar.

MRS. BATALI'S BANANA CHOCOLATE CHIP BARS

Marilyn Batali of Salumi and Mario Batali of Babbo

This recipe, a favorite childhood dessert of Chef Mario Batali, was created by his mother, Marilyn. The intriguing flavor combination of bananas, cinnamon, and chocolate chips is delightful. • MAKES 24 SERVINGS

6 ounces (1½ sticks) unsalted butter, softened, plus more for the pan

2 cups all-purpose flour

2 teaspoons baking powder

1 teaspoon salt

½ teaspoon ground cinnamon

⅓ cup granulated sugar

1 cup packed light brown sugar

1 large egg

1 teaspoon pure vanilla extract

1 cup mashed ripe bananas (3 to 4)

12 ounces (2 cups) bittersweet chocolate chunks

Confectioners' sugar, for dusting

Preheat the oven to 350°F. Butter a half-sheet pan, and set aside.

In a medium bowl, whisk together the flour, baking powder, salt, and cinnamon, and set aside.

In the bowl of a stand mixer fitted with the paddle attachment, cream the butter, granulated sugar, and brown sugar. Add the egg and continue to beat until fluffy. Add the vanilla, then the bananas, then the dry ingredients, and mix just until combined. With a silicone spatula, fold in the chocolate chunks.

Spread the batter evenly in the prepared pan. Bake for 20 to 25 minutes, until the edges are golden brown and the center springs back when pressed gently. Remove the cake from the oven, and let cool completely in the pan. Sift confectioners' sugar over the top and slice into 24 rectangles.

CHOCOLATE CHIP WALNUT COFFEE CAKE

Tracy Obolsky of North End Grill

Pastry chef Obolsky told me, "This coffee cake is my grandmother's original recipe. She was a phenomenal baker. I have a copy of her recipe, typed on a typewriter, which I think is really cool. Whenever I cook from her recipes, I feel like I am somehow connecting with her. The addition of the chocolate chips was my spin on her delicious classic." · MAKES 12 SERVINGS

8 ounces (2 sticks) unsalted butter, softened, plus more for the pan

1½ cups granulated sugar, divided

½ cup packed dark brown sugar

½ teaspoon ground cinnamon

1 cup chopped walnuts

3 cups all-purpose flour

4 teaspoons baking powder

1 teaspoon baking soda

1½ teaspoons salt

4 large eggs, at room temperature

1 cup sour cream

1 teaspoon pure vanilla extract

6 ounces (1 cup) bittersweet or semisweet chocolate chips

Preheat the oven to 325°F. Butter a tube pan, and set aside.

To make the topping: In a large bowl, mix together ½ cup of granulated sugar, brown sugar, cinnamon, and walnuts, and set aside.

In a medium bowl, combine the flour, baking powder, baking soda, and salt, and set aside.

In the bowl of a stand mixer, cream the butter and the remaining 1 cup of granulated sugar until light and fluffy. Add the eggs, one at a time. Add the sour cream and vanilla. Add the flour mixture. Add the chocolate chips.

Spread half of the batter evenly into the prepared pan. Sprinkle half of the cinnamon walnut topping over the batter. Top with the remaining batter, then sprinkle the remaining topping over the cake. Bake for 55 minutes, or until firm. Remove the cake from the oven, and let cool in the pan for 10 minutes; then remove the cake from the pan, and cool completely.

CHOCOLATE CHIP BUTTERMILK CAKE

Elisa Strauss of Confetti Cakes

This scrumptious cake came into being because pastry chef Strauss's husband asked her for a poppy seed cake without lemon. She toyed with the recipe, eliminating the lemon and poppy seeds, to create a chocolate chip treat.

• MAKES 12 SERVINGS

8 ounces (2 sticks) unsalted butter, softened, plus more for the pan

2 cups all-purpose flour, plus more for dusting the pan

½ teaspoon salt

2½ teaspoons baking powder

1 cup granulated sugar

1 cup packed light brown sugar

3 large eggs, separated

1 cup buttermilk

2 teaspoons pure vanilla bean paste

6 ounces (1 cup) bittersweet or semisweet chocolate chips

Confectioners' sugar, for dusting

Preheat the oven to 350°F. Butter a 10-inch Bundt or tube pan, lightly dust it with flour, and set aside.

In a large bowl, combine the flour, salt, and baking powder, and set aside.

In the bowl of a stand mixer fitted with the paddle attachment, cream together the butter, granulated sugar, and brown sugar. Once combined, add the egg yolks, one at a time. Scrape down the sides of the bowl. Slowly add the buttermilk and vanilla, and beat until smooth. Gradually add the dry ingredients, in three additions, mix well, and set aside.

Place a clean bowl in the mixer fitted with the whip attachment. Whisk the egg whites until stiff and shiny. Be careful not to overwhip. With a silicone spatula, gently fold the egg whites into the batter. Gently fold in the chocolate chips.

Spread the mixture into the prepared pan. Bake in the center of the oven for about 45 minutes, or until a toothpick inserted into the center comes out clean. Remove the cake from the oven, cool for about 20 minutes in the pan, then turn out onto a cake plate. Dust with sifted confectioners' sugar.

NONNA'S DARK CHOCOLATE CAKE WITH WHIPPED CREAM

Micol Negrin of Rustico Cooking

"My Nonna Eva was not really a baker; she was more of a savory cook, and quite an incredible one at that. However, when my father and his two brothers were growing up in Tangiers, and later Milan, she baked this cake daily," Chef Negrin told me. "The three brothers would arrive home from school famished and polish off the whole cake within minutes. Despite the speed with which my dad and uncles ate this cake, it keeps perfectly for days, wrapped in plastic at room temperature. The use of cinnamon and grated lemon zest in this chocolate cake hints at my grandmother's Turkish roots." · MAKES 10 SERVINGS

Nonstick cooking spray

1¼ cups granulated sugar, plus more
    for coating the pan

1¼ cups all-purpose flour

1 cup natural cocoa powder, sifted

1 envelope Italian vanilla-scented
    baking powder

½ teaspoon ground cinnamon

⅛ teaspoon fine sea salt

7 tablespoons unsalted butter,
    softened

Grated zest of 1 lemon

2 large eggs

1 cup whole milk

3 ounces (½ cup) mini chocolate chips

Confectioners' sugar, for dusting

Preheat the oven to 325°F (preferably set on convection). Lightly spray a 10-inch Bundt pan with nonstick cooking spray and coat with granulated sugar. Tap out the excess sugar, and set aside.

Into a medium bowl, sift together the flour, cocoa powder, baking powder, cinnamon, and salt, and whisk to combine. Set aside.

In the bowl of a stand mixer fitted with the whip attachment, beat the butter with the remaining 1¼ cups of the granulated sugar and lemon zest on medium speed until pale and light, about 5 minutes. The sugar should not be visibly grainy any longer and the mixture will have lightened quite a bit. Add the eggs, one at a time, with the mixer on low speed, and mix until combined and fluffy.

Add half of the dry ingredients, then add the milk, and finally add the remaining dry ingredients. Mix until the batter is uniformly dark and lump free. Do not overbeat or the finished cake will be tough. With a silicone spatula, gently fold in the chocolate chips.

Spoon the batter into the prepared pan. Bake in the middle of the oven for 45 minutes, or until a cake tester or toothpick inserted into the center comes out clean. Remove the cake from the oven, and cool in the pan for 5 minutes. Turn out onto a wire rack to cool completely, with the top facing up so that it does not become marked by the rack. Dust with sifted confectioners' sugar. Serve the cake in thick slices, with a tuft of whipped cream.

NOTE: Instead of Italian baking powder (such as Lievito Pane degli Angeli), substitute 1½ teaspoons baking powder plus 1 teaspoon pure vanilla extract.

WHIPPED CREAM

1 cup heavy cream

1 tablespoon confectioners' sugar

1 teaspoon pure vanilla extract

In a clean bowl of a stand mixer fitted with a clean whip attachment, whip the cream to the soft-peak stage, then add the confectioners' sugar and vanilla.

CHOCOLATE CHIP GUGELHUPF

Alexander Grunert of Chef's Table at Brooklyn Fare

A *gugelhupf* (or *kugelhopf*) is beloved in Chef Grunert's native Austria. It is traditionally made in an earthenware or copper mold, but you can use your trusty Bundt pan instead. My boys like a slice of the chef's cake, toasted, for a sweet breakfast. · MAKES 12 SERVINGS

8 ounces (2 sticks) unsalted butter, softened, plus more for the pan

½ cup sliced almonds, for the pan

¼ cup cornstarch

¼ cup confectioners' sugar, plus more for dusting

1 teaspoon pure vanilla extract

Pinch of salt

5 large egg yolks

1⅓ cups pastry flour

4 large egg whites

⅔ cup granulated sugar

6 ounces (1 cup) bittersweet or semisweet chocolate chips

Preheat the oven to 325°F. Butter a 10-inch Bundt or tube pan, coat with the sliced almonds, and set aside.

In the bowl of a stand mixer fitted with the paddle attachment, cream the butter, cornstarch, confectioners' sugar, vanilla, and salt. Add the egg yolks, one at a time, and mix to incorporate. With a silicone spatula, gently fold in the flour, just until incorporated, and set aside.

In the clean bowl of the stand mixer fitted with the whip attachment, whisk the egg whites until foamy. On medium speed, slowly add the granulated sugar, 1 tablespoon at a time, and beat until stiff peaks form. With a silicone spatula, gently fold in the butter-egg mixture, just until incorporated. Gently fold in the chocolate chips.

Fill the Bundt pan with batter, and even the top with an offset spatula. Bake for 40 to 45 minutes, until golden brown. Remove the cake from the oven, let cool in the pan for 5 minutes, then unmold. Cool completely on a wire rack. Dust with confectioners' sugar.

CHOCOLATE CHIP FINANCIERS

Michael Laiskonis of the Institute of Culinary Education

These pastries, said to resemble gold bars, were sold near the Paris Bourse (stock exchange). Pastry chef Laiskonis says, "Financiers have long been among my favorite French pastries, and I've continued to adapt the classic idea over the years to come up with new versions. This one, with the simple addition of ground chocolate chips, intensifies the financiers' nutty aroma and dense, moist interior. The browned butter used in the recipe is a large part of what defines the classic financier; the darker the color, the deeper the flavor, but exercise caution to avoid cooking the solids too far, as blackened butter will result in a bitter, burned flavor." · MAKES 12 TO 24 SMALL CAKES

4 ounces (1 stick) unsalted butter

10 tablespoons almond flour

½ cup all-purpose flour

1 cup plus 3 tablespoons
    confectioners' sugar

4 large egg whites

3 ounces (½ cup) bittersweet or
    semisweet chocolate chips, frozen

Nonstick cooking spray

In a small, heavy saucepan, gently melt and cook the butter, whisking continuously, to a light brown color. Remove the saucepan from the heat just as the butter begins to brown in order to avoid burning it. Set aside, and let the butter cool to room temperature.

In a medium bowl, thoroughly combine the almond flour, all-purpose flour, and confectioners' sugar.

In a second medium bowl, using a whisk, whip the egg whites just until frothy and the yellow color dissipates. Whisk in the dry ingredients. Slowly whisk in the brown butter, stirring until fully incorporated. Cover with plastic wrap and chill for 30 minutes. This important step will allow the flour to fully hydrate and firm up the batter, making it easier to portion.

Meanwhile, place the frozen chocolate chips in a blender or food processor fitted with the metal blade, and lightly pulse to break the chips into smaller pieces; running the blender or processor too long may heat the chips, causing them to melt. With a silicone spatula, fold the ground chocolate chips into the chilled financier batter.

Preheat the oven to 325°F. Lightly spray mini muffin tins or silicone molds with nonstick cooking spray. Using a small scoop, spoon, or pastry bag, transfer the mixture to the prepared tins. Bake for 20 to 25 minutes, until golden brown at the edges. Remove the cakes from the oven, and let cool slightly before removing them from the muffin tins or molds.

CHOCOLATE CHIP MADELEINES

Daniel Boulud of Daniel

Chef Boulud told me, "Warm, ethereal madeleines have been an integral part of my restaurant's menus. It is the finishing touch of my patrons' meals, and often the most memorable. When we opened Épicerie Boulud, my gourmet takeout food shop on the Upper West Side, we knew we had to include this favorite dessert. This recipe is slightly altered from our restaurant version into a larger size madeleine with a slightly cakier texture that remains moist. We decided to add chocolate chips, because who doesn't love chocolate chips?" You will need a large nonstick madeleine pan for this recipe. • MAKES 24 CAKES

1 cup granulated sugar

4 large eggs

2 cups all-purpose flour

2½ teaspoons baking powder

9 ounces (2¼ sticks) unsalted butter

⅓ cup milk, cold

½ teaspoon pure vanilla extract

Nonstick cooking spray

3 ounces (½ cup) dark chocolate chips

In the bowl of a stand mixer fitted with the paddle attachment, mix the sugar and eggs until airy, and set aside.

In a medium bowl, whisk together the flour and baking powder, then gradually stream this mixture into the egg mixture on low speed. Increase the speed to medium and beat for 30 seconds.

In a small saucepan, melt the butter, and while still warm, with the mixer running on low, stream the butter into the batter. Mix in the milk and vanilla until well combined. Cover the batter with plastic wrap and let rest overnight, or at least 3 hours in the refrigerator. Transfer to piping bags.

Preheat the oven to 375°F. Liberally spray the madeleine pan with nonstick cooking spray. Line a half-sheet pan with parchment paper, and set aside.

Pipe the madeleines into the prepared cavities of the madeleine pan, and fill to the rim. Sprinkle 10 to 15 chocolate chips on each cookie. Bake for 3 minutes, rotate the pan 180 degrees, and then reduce the heat to 325°F. Bake for another

8 minutes, or until cooked through (the edges will turn golden brown and the centers will rise). Remove the madeleine pan from the oven. Tap the hot mold over the prepared half-sheet pan so the madeleines drop out. Repeat with the remaining batter. Serve either warm or cool.

PUMPKIN CHOCOLATE CHIP BREAD

Amanda Cook of Tenth Avenue Cookshop

When pastry chef Cook was around eight years old, her mother gave her a pumpkin chocolate chip muffin. She loved the delightful combination of the spicy cake and the dark chocolate chips that "just sang together in harmony." Here is her adaption of this favorite recipe. You can use loaf pans or any shape disposable paper molds. Less baking time may be required for paper molds.

• MAKES 3 LOAVES

Nonstick cooking spray

3¼ cups all-purpose flour

2 teaspoons baking soda

1 teaspoon baking powder

1½ teaspoons ground cinnamon

1 teaspoon ground nutmeg

1 teaspoon ground ginger

½ teaspoon ground cloves

3 cups granulated sugar

1 cup canola or vegetable oil

4 large eggs

1½ cups pumpkin puree

9 ounces (1½ cups) bittersweet or
semisweet chocolate chips

Preheat the oven to 350°F. Lightly spray three 8-inch loaf pans with nonstick cooking spray, and set aside.

Into a medium bowl, sift together the flour, baking soda, baking powder, cinnamon, nutmeg, ginger, and cloves, and set aside.

In the bowl of a stand mixer fitted with the paddle attachment, beat the sugar, oil, and eggs together until the mixture is pale yellow and ribbons form. Add the pumpkin and blend well. Add the dry ingredients, and mix just until combined. With a silicone spatula, fold in the chocolate chips.

Divide the batter evenly among the prepared pans. Bake for 35 to 45 minutes, until the center of each cake tests clean with a toothpick. Remove the loaves from the oven, and let cool in the pans.

CHOCOLATE CHIP ZUCCHINI CAKE

Jessamyn Rodriguez of Hot Bread Kitchen

Jessamyn Rodriguez sometimes glazes her cake with a cream cheese frosting. "This is a moist and rich cake made with olive oil, plenty of chocolate chips, and zucchini," she says. "Since it has veggies in it, I convince myself that it is healthy and I feed it without guilt to my kids. Glaze it with chocolate and you can even throw some candles on it for a subversively healthy birthday cake."

• MAKES ABOUT 12 SERVINGS

Nonstick cooking spray or butter

2 cups all-purpose flour

2 teaspoons baking soda

1 teaspoon baking powder

¾ teaspoon salt

2 teaspoons ground cinnamon

3 large eggs

2 cups granulated sugar

1 cup olive oil

2 cups coarsely grated zucchini

9 ounces (1½ cups) dark chocolate chips, plus ¼ cup for melting

1 cup chopped walnuts (optional)

Confectioners' sugar, for dusting

Preheat the oven to 350°F. Lightly coat a 12-cup Bundt pan with nonstick cooking spray or butter, and set aside.

In a large mixing bowl, whisk together the flour, baking soda, baking powder, salt, and cinnamon, and set aside.

In the bowl of a stand mixer fitted with the paddle attachment or a food processor fitted with the steel blade, blend the eggs and granulated sugar. Add the oil gradually, and whip until light in color. Using a spatula, mix in the dry ingredients, just until combined. Mix in the zucchini. Fold in 1½ cups of the chocolate chips and nuts (if using).

Pour the batter into the pan. Bake for 50 to 60 minutes, until the cake is baked through. Cool for 20 minutes in the pan, and then invert onto a cooling rack. When the cake is completely cooled, dust it with confectioners' sugar. Melt the reserved ¼ cup chocolate chips, and drizzle on top for a glaze.

HONEY CAKE

Joan Nathan

Here is my version of culinary historian Joan Nathan's beloved honey cake. Sometimes I personalize it with chocolate chips. Joan thankfully approves.

• MAKES 2 LOAVES

Butter, for the pans

3½ cups all-purpose flour, plus more for the pans

1 cup strong brewed coffee

1¾ cups honey

4 large eggs

¼ cup vegetable oil

1¼ cups packed dark brown sugar

1 tablespoon baking powder

1 teaspoon baking soda

1 teaspoon cinnamon

¼ teaspoon ground cloves

¼ teaspoon ground nutmeg

½ teaspoon ground ginger

½ cup chopped toasted almonds or walnuts

6 ounces (1 cup) bittersweet or semisweet chocolate chips

Preheat the oven to 300°F. Generously butter and flour two 9 by 5–inch loaf pans, and set aside.

In a 2-quart saucepan, combine the coffee and honey, and bring to a boil. Let cool, and set aside.

In a large mixing bowl, with a wooden spoon, beat the eggs. Stir in the oil and brown sugar, and set aside.

Into another large mixing bowl, sift together the flour, baking powder, baking soda, cinnamon, cloves, nutmeg, and ginger. Fold in the nuts and chocolate chips.

Stir the flour mixture and honey mixture alternately into the egg mixture until fully combined.

Pour the batter into the loaf pans. Bake for 70 minutes, or until the cakes are springy to the touch. Remove the cakes from the oven, and let cool completely. Do not serve for 24 hours, so that the flavor of the honey has a chance to develop.

ITALIAN OLIVE OIL CAKE WITH CHOCOLATE CHIPS
Giuseppa

A couple of summers ago, my friend Annie invited me to lunch at her friend's farmhouse in Italy. This cake was served for dessert. Our hostess, Giuseppa, noticed how much I loved it and gave me her recipe, in Italian, scrawled on a napkin. I made it the very first day I returned home to New York City. Because my Italian is spotty—I speak enough to get into trouble, but not enough to get out of it (thanks, Mamma and Nonnie)—I was thrilled that the cake turned out exactly as the one we shared on that memorable day. • MAKES 2 LOAVES

1 cup olive oil, plus more for the pans
2 cups granulated sugar
3 large eggs
1 cup whole milk
Grated zest of 1 lemon
2¾ cups all-purpose flour

1 envelope Italian vanilla-scented
    baking powder
2 tablespoons bittersweet chocolate
    chips or coarsely chopped
    bittersweet chocolate

Preheat the oven to 350°F. Oil two 9 by 5–inch loaf pans, and set aside.

In the bowl of a stand mixer fitted with the paddle attachment, beat the sugar and eggs until a ribbon forms, about 3 minutes. Add the remaining 1 cup of olive oil, milk, and lemon zest. Add the flour and baking powder, and mix just until combined. With a silicone spatula, fold in the chocolate chips.

Scrape the batter into the prepared pans. Bake for 40 to 50 minutes, until golden. Remove the cakes from the oven, cool for about 20 minutes in the pans, then remove the cakes from the pans, and let cool completely on a wire rack.

NOTE: Instead of Italian baking powder (such as Lievito Pane degli Angeli), substitute 1½ teaspoons baking powder plus 1 teaspoon pure vanilla extract.

CHAPTER

*№*4

FANCY CAKES

CHOCOLATE BLACKOUT CAKE

Alina Martell Acosta of Ai Fiori

Pastry chef Acosta says, "To the best of my knowledge there is no recipe out there for the iconic Brooklyn blackout cake from the legendary Ebinger's bakery. The bakery never shared the recipe. The cake, according to everyone who loved it, was intensely chocolate—with three layers of devil's food cake and a pudding-like chocolate filling—frosted with a dark chocolate ganache, and coated in cake crumbs. The name comes from a time during World War II when New York City used to run blackout drills, which allowed ships to exit the harbor in the dark, protecting them from enemy ships and planes. I have tried several versions, and the more chocolate I add, the better it gets. Although chocolate chips are not part of the original recipe, they add texture inside the cake and all of the chocolate bits on the outside make for a very pretty cake." • MAKES ABOUT 12 SLICES

DEVIL'S FOOD CAKE

1½ cups cake flour	10 large egg yolks
½ cup Dutch-process cocoa powder	⅞ cup water
½ cup black cocoa powder	1⅛ cups grapeseed oil
¼ teaspoon baking soda	2¼ cups granulated sugar, divided
2 teaspoons baking powder	12 large egg whites

Preheat the oven to 350°F. Line three half-sheet pans with a Silpat (or spray nonstick cooking spray on three half-sheet pans, line each with parchment paper, and then spray the parchment), and set aside.

Into a medium bowl, sift together the cake flour, Dutch-process cocoa powder, black cocoa powder, baking soda, and baking powder, and set aside.

In the bowl of a stand mixer fitted with the whip attachment, combine the egg yolks, water, and oil until homogenous. Add 1½ cups of the sugar to the yolk mixture, and whisk until combined. Add the dry ingredients, and whisk for 5 minutes. The mixture should be smooth and shiny without any lumps. Set the mixture aside.

In a clean bowl of a stand mixer fitted with a clean whip attachment, begin to whip the egg whites on medium speed. Add the remaining ¾ cup sugar, 1 tablespoon at a time, and whip until medium peaks form. With a silicone spatula, fold a small amount of the meringue into the cake batter, then gently fold all of the cake batter into the remaining meringue.

Spread the batter evenly onto the half-sheet pans. Bake for 20 to 25 minutes, rotating the pans halfway through baking, until the cakes begin to pull away from the sides and the centers spring back to the touch. Remove the cakes from the oven, and let cool to room temperature. Remove the cakes from the pans, and allow them to cool completely. Place them, covered with plastic wrap, in the refrigerator until you are ready to assemble the cake.

CHOCOLATE CHIP PASTRY CREAM

⅔ cup granulated sugar

1 large egg

2 large egg yolks

¼ cup cornstarch

3 tablespoons Dutch-process cocoa powder

2 cups whole milk

3 ounces Valrhona Guanaja 70 percent dark chocolate, melted

4½ ounces (¾ cup) chopped Valrhona Guanaja 70 percent dark chocolate or mini dark chocolate chips

Line a half-sheet pan with plastic wrap, and set aside.

In a medium bowl, mix together the sugar, egg, egg yolks, cornstarch, and cocoa powder. Whisk the mixture until the sugar is dissolved, and set aside.

In a medium saucepan, heat the milk until it is warm. Add a small amount of the milk to the egg mixture to temper. Add the egg mixture to the milk, and cook until the mixture thickens and just begins to boil. Take off the heat, and add the melted chocolate. Whisk well or blend using a hand blender. Pour out onto the prepared pan. Press another sheet of plastic wrap onto the surface of the pastry cream. Refrigerate for 1 hour.

In the bowl of a stand mixer fitted with the paddle attachment, beat the chilled pastry cream until smooth. Add the chopped chocolate, and set aside.

CHOCOLATE GLAZE

3 sheets leaf gelatin (silver strength)

1¼ cups heavy cream

⅔ cup water

⅓ cup granulated sugar

⅓ cup glucose syrup or corn syrup

18 ounces Valrhona Guanaja 70 percent dark chocolate, melted

Bloom or soften the gelatin in a medium bowl of ice water for about 10 minutes. In a small saucepan, heat the cream, water, sugar, and glucose syrup, and set the saucepan aside. In the top of a double boiler, over medium heat, melt the chocolate, and set aside.

Bring the cream mixture in the saucepan to a boil, remove from the heat, and set aside. Remove the gelatin from the ice water, and gently wring it out with your hands. Add the gelatin to the cream mixture. Strain these liquids over the chocolate, whisk to combine, and cool for 5 minutes.

NOTE: This mixture can be chilled completely and reheated for later use.

CRUMB DECORATIONS

Reserved chocolate cake crumbs

Finely chopped Valrhona Guanaja 70 percent dark chocolate

Valrhona dark chocolate pearls

Any combination of chocolate sprinkles, shards of tempered chocolate, cocoa nibs, chocolate shavings, and mini chocolate chips

Toss together the cake crumbs, chopped chocolate, chocolate pearls, and any other decorations, and set aside. Using an 8-inch cake pan or cardboard cake round, cut out five 8-inch rounds from the 3 cakes. Save all of the scraps; turn them into crumbs.

To assemble the cake: Place one 8-inch cake on a cake round. Pipe or spread a layer of chocolate chip pastry cream on the cake round. Place another cake on top, spread another layer of pastry cream on top, and repeat for each cake layer. With a metal offset spatula, smooth out the sides of the cake so the edges are clean. Refrigerate until the pastry cream is firm.

Place the chilled cake on a cooling rack over a half-sheet pan lined with parchment paper. Pour the warmed chocolate glaze over the top of the cake, allowing it to run down and cover all the sides. Smooth out the sides and top. Refrigerate until the glaze is set.

Remove the cake from the cooling rack, and press the reserved crumb decorations onto the sides of the cake.

CHOCOLATE TRUFFLE CAKE

Vivie and David Glass of David Glass Chocolates

This beloved cake was sold at Zabar's for many years. I always dreamed of making it myself. I now often bake two, or even four. Bakers Vivie and David Glass were so sweet to indulge me by allowing the addition of chocolate chips to their perfect recipe. The cake is eaten at room temperature, or even better—wrap it in plastic wrap and place it in the refrigerator for a few hours. That's how the Zabar boys like it. · MAKES ABOUT 6 SERVINGS

Nonstick cooking spray

3½ ounces (scant ½ cup) semisweet chocolate chips

½ ounce unsweetened chocolate, cut into small pieces

4 ounces (1 stick) unsalted butter, cut into small pieces

2 extra-large eggs

½ cup granulated sugar

2 tablespoons sifted Dutch-process cocoa powder

3 ounces (½ cup) bittersweet chocolate chips

Grease a solid-bottom, 6-inch cake pan with nonstick cooking spray, making sure to hit every spot, and set aside.

Preheat the oven to 350°F. Carefully place a 9 by 13–inch cake pan in the oven. Fill it with hot water so the pan is filled about one-third of the way up. Let the water heat while you prepare the batter.

In the top of a double boiler over medium-low heat, melt the semisweet chocolate chips, unsweetened chocolate, and butter together, stirring with a whisk until the mixture is absolutely smooth.

Meanwhile, put the whip attachment on a stand mixer. In the bowl of the mixer, combine the eggs and sugar on medium speed until well incorporated. You don't want to mix this on high speed or for too long or the cake will not have the proper texture. Mix it enough so that when you rub a bit of the eggs and sugar between your fingers, the sugar feels dissolved. Pour the melted chocolate mixture into the egg mixture. Beat on medium until fully incorporated.

Add the cocoa powder on low speed. When the cocoa disappears, turn the mixer to high speed briefly to make sure it is thoroughly mixed in. With a silicone spatula, fold in the chocolate chips.

Pour the batter into the prepared 6-inch pan. Carefully place the pan into the 9 by 13–inch pan that is in the oven. Check the level of hot water: It should come halfway up the side of the cake pan. If it does not, add a little more water. Do not let the cake pan float.

Bake for 55 minutes to 1 hour. The top of the cake should have formed a paper-thin crust and will have cracked slightly in the center. Remove the cake from the oven, and let it cool to lukewarm. Place a 6-inch cardboard cake round over the cake and, gripping the pan and the cake round, flip the cake over. Rap the edge of the pan sharply one or two times on a countertop. The cake will come out easily. Cool completely on a wire rack. Cut into 6 slices.

ZEBRA CAKE

Tracey Zabar

This classic icebox cake, with chocolate chips strewn on top, consists of soft, rich cookies, glued together with a huge amount of whipped cream. The cake is placed in the refrigerator (or icebox) to allow the cookies to absorb the cream, and the cake to firm up. When you cut the cake at an angle, stripes of a zebra show. This messy, yummy dessert doesn't travel well, but it's a home run when you place it on the table in front of anyone with a sweet tooth. · MAKES 12 SERVINGS

COOKIES

6 ounces (1½ sticks) unsalted butter, softened

1¼ cups granulated sugar

1 large egg

1 teaspoon pure vanilla bean paste

1½ cups all-purpose flour

¼ cup Dutch-process cocoa powder, sifted

½ teaspoon salt

In the bowl of a stand mixer fitted with the paddle attachment, cream the butter and sugar. Add the egg, then the vanilla bean paste. Add the flour, cocoa powder, and salt, and mix just until combined. Place the batter on a piece of parchment paper, form it into a log, and tightly roll the paper around the log. Place in the freezer for 1 hour.

Preheat the oven to 350°F. Line a half-sheet pan with parchment paper, and set aside.

Slice the log into sixteen ½-inch rounds, and place on the prepared pan. Bake for 12 to 14 minutes, until the center of each cookie appears firm. Remove the cookies from the oven, and let cool completely on the pan.

1 cup heavy cream

3 tablespoons granulated sugar

½ teaspoon pure vanilla extract

¼ cup mini chocolate chips

In the bowl of a stand mixer fitted with the whip attachment (make sure that the bowl and whisk are perfectly clean and grease free), start to whip the cream. Very slowly add the sugar, then the vanilla, and whip just until stiff peaks form. Do not overwhip.

To assemble the cake: Place a cookie on a platter. With a silicone spatula, place about ½ tablespoon whipped cream on top. Place another cookie on top of the cream. Repeat with the remaining cookies, using about half of the cream in all. Carefully lift the stack of cookies and cream, and lay it down sideways on the platter. Place the remaining whipped cream on the top and sides of the cake, forming a rough loaf, and sprinkle the chocolate chips on top.

Place the platter, loosely covered with plastic wrap, in the refrigerator for 1 hour to allow the cookies to soften. Slice at an angle, and serve cold.

MOCHA ROULADE

Cara Tannenbaum of the Institute of Culinary Education

Chef Tannenbaum's mocha roulade is a flourless wonder. Originally basing her recipe on Dione Lucas's (a beloved cookbook icon who wrote about French cooking before Julia Child did) roulade recipe, Chef Tannenbaum has changed the proportions over the years. What is also new is its knockout flavor due to the hints of espresso and chocolate chips in the whipped cream. The roulade is quite easy to make: Just follow the directions exactly and you will have a fabulous ending to your next dinner party. • MAKES 12 SERVINGS

ROULADE

Unsalted butter, softened, for the pan

12 large eggs, separated

2¼ cups plus 2 tablespoons superfine
 sugar, divided

1 cup Dutch-process cocoa powder,
 sifted

Preheat the oven to 400°F. Line a half-sheet pan with a piece of parchment paper large enough to go up the sides and over the edges of the pan by 1 inch. Butter the parchment, and set aside.

In the bowl of a stand mixer fitted with the whip attachment, whisk the egg yolks on medium speed until they begin to thicken. Gradually add 1½ cups of the sugar, and continue to whip the yolks until they are very thick, increased in volume, and lemon colored, about 5 minutes. Set them aside in a large bowl, and clean the mixer bowl and whip attachment.

In the clean bowl of the stand mixer refitted with the clean whip, whisk the egg whites at medium-high speed until they are frothy and foamy. Gradually add the remaining ¾ cup sugar, reserving 2 tablespoons. Whip until stiff (but not dry) peaks form, about 3 minutes.

Sift the cocoa powder onto the egg yolks, and, using a silicone spatula, fold it in. Add one-quarter of the whipped whites, and stir to mix. In three additions, gently fold in the remaining whites, just until combined.

Pour into the prepared pan, and spread with an offset spatula, being careful not to deflate the mixture. Bake for 17 to 19 minutes, until well risen and firm. Remove the cake from the oven, and immediately sprinkle 2 tablespoons of the remaining sugar on top. As the cake cools, it will deflate like a soufflé, and that is fine. Allow it to cool completely on the pan.

MELTED CHOCOLATE AND MOCHA CREAM

6 ounces (1 cup) mini chocolate chips, divided

2 teaspoons instant espresso powder

2 tablespoons water

2 cups heavy cream

2 tablespoons superfine sugar, plus more for dusting

2 teaspoons pure vanilla extract

In a small bowl over a pot of simmering water, melt ½ cup of the chocolate chips with the espresso powder and water. Remove from the heat and set aside to cool.

In the bowl of a stand mixer fitted with the whip attachment, whip the heavy cream until thickened, and add the sugar and vanilla. Beat until soft peaks form. Gently fold in the remaining ½ cup chocolate chips.

To assemble the roulade: Trim the top and bottom edges of the cake, and discard them. Place a 24-inch length of heavy-duty aluminum foil on your counter, and flip the cake out, sugared side down, onto the foil. Remove the parchment paper.

Spread the cooled, melted chocolate evenly over the cake. Spread the whipped cream over the chocolate to within ½ inch of the edges.

Lifting the foil from the top of the cake, carefully and tightly roll the cake toward you. When the cake is completely rolled, fold the top edges of the foil together to close the package, and twist the ends to seal. Refrigerate for 2 hours, or up to 24 hours.

When you are ready to serve, open the ends of the foil, and place the cake onto a serving platter with the seam side down. Trim the uneven edges off each end of the cake, and cut the cake into 1½-inch slices. Dust with superfine sugar.

NOTE: If you freeze the roulade, it will taste like ice-cream cake.

PINGUINO (PENGUIN CAKE)

Tracey Zabar

Our family birthday cake's original recipe for devil's food cake came from a 1950s ladies' magazine and it has evolved over the years. I slather gobs of ganache or Nutella in between the layers and add chocolate chips. At one celebration, we watched, helplessly, as the top layer of this cake slowly slid to the floor. We were too far across the room to catch it. The children screamed, my husband laughed, and the dog needed to be carried out of the room. I threw it in the trash, wiped the floor, and knew there was going to be a good story there . . . some day. The kids call this cake "The One that Fell on the Floor," but I call it *pinguino*, as a similarly named torta was often served at Italian children's birthday parties when I worked in Italy. The Italians add whipped cream to make it match a penguin's tuxedo; so we now do, too. · MAKES 8 SERVINGS

PINGUINO

6 ounces (1½ sticks) unsalted butter, softened, plus more for the pans

1¼ cups granulated sugar, plus more for the pans

½ cup Dutch-process cocoa powder

½ cup boiling water

1½ cups all-purpose flour

1 teaspoon baking powder

½ teaspoon salt

½ cup sour cream

2 large eggs

1 teaspoon pure vanilla bean paste

3 ounces (½ cup) bittersweet chocolate chips

½ cup Nutella, for frosting the cake

Preheat the oven to 350°F. Butter the sides of four 4-inch or two 8-inch round cake pans. Sprinkle a few teaspoons of sugar into each pan, swirl so the sugar sticks to the butter, turn the pans upside down over the trash, and tap to discard the excess sugar. Place a parchment round in the bottom of each pan, and set aside.

In a small, heat-proof bowl, combine the cocoa powder and water, and set aside to cool for 5 minutes.

In a medium bowl, whisk together the flour, baking powder, and salt, and set aside.

In the bowl of a stand mixer fitted with the paddle attachment, cream the butter and the remaining 1¼ cups of sugar. Add the sour cream, eggs, vanilla, and cocoa mixture. Add the dry ingredients, and mix just until combined. With a silicone spatula, gently fold in the chocolate chips.

Place the batter in the prepared pans. Bake for 25 to 30 minutes, until the cakes spring back when gently touched (be careful, they're hot!) with your hand. Remove the cakes from the oven, cool for 10 minutes, then remove them from the pans, and let cool completely on a wire rack.

WHIPPED CREAM

1 cup heavy cream

1 teaspoon pure vanilla bean paste

3 tablespoons granulated sugar

2 tablespoons confectioners' sugar, for dusting

In the bowl of a stand mixer fitted with a clean whip attachment, whip the cream and vanilla. Very slowly add the sugar and whip just until stiff peaks form.

To assemble the *pinguino*: Place a layer of the cake on a flat plate. Spread the Nutella on top, then slather a thick layer of whipped cream on top of the Nutella. Place the second layer on top. Dust with confectioners' sugar.

ANGEL FOOD CAKE WITH MINI CHOCOLATE CHIPS

Maida Heatter

When I was a young bride, I pored over Maida Heatter's baking books. Following her directions exactly, I felt as if I were getting a degree in baking from the master. Thirty years later, thanks to our mutual friend, Nick Malgieri, we now know each other. When she gave me this recipe, I asked Nick if the cake would rise (angel food cakes climb up the sides of the always ungreased pan) with the addition of chocolate chips. He said, "Put the cake in the oven, get down on your knees, and pray it doesn't fall." Maida said to try it. I'm so glad I did, as the result is divine. · MAKES ABOUT 12 SERVINGS

1 cup cake flour

1½ cups superfine sugar, divided

16 large egg whites

½ teaspoon salt

1½ teaspoons cream of tartar

2 teaspoons pure vanilla extract

3 ounces (½ cup) mini chocolate chips

Preheat the oven to 375°F. Set aside a 10-inch angel food pan (not nonstick).

In a medium bowl, sift together, four times, the cake flour and ¾ cup of the sugar, and set aside.

In the bowl of a stand mixer fitted with the whip attachment (make sure bowl and whip are perfectly clean and grease free), beat the egg whites on medium speed for 1 minute. Add the salt, cream of tartar, and vanilla. Increase the speed to high, and beat until the mixture holds a soft shape. Reduce the speed to medium and add the remaining ¾ cup sugar, 1 tablespoon at a time, then increase the speed to high again, and beat until the whites hold a firm peak when the whip is raised, but are not shiny and dry. With a silicone spatula, gently transfer the egg whites into a large 8-quart bowl, and gently fold in the dry ingredients, just until incorporated. Gently fold in the chocolate chips.

Turn the batter into the cake pan and cut through the cake with a thin metal spatula to eliminate any large air pockets, and smooth the top. Bake for about 45 minutes, or until the cake springs back when gently touched with a fingertip. Remove the pan from the oven and invert it. If the pan does not have metal feet to keep the cake raised from the surface, hang it upside down on top of an empty glass wine bottle. Cool the cake completely in the inverted pan. Slide a thin knife around the edges to release the cake from the pan.

NOTE: If you don't have superfine sugar, place granulated sugar in a food processor fitted with the metal blade and pulse for about 30 seconds.

VANILLA CHIP CUPCAKES

Tracey Zabar

These darling cupcakes, sprinkled with chips, are buttery delights. Dress them up with a shiny ganache frosting, and add a sugared violet on top of each cupcake.

• MAKES 12 LARGE (OR 24 SMALL) CUPCAKES

1½ cups all-purpose flour

1 teaspoon baking powder

½ teaspoon salt

6 ounces (1½ sticks) unsalted butter, softened

1 cup granulated sugar

3 large eggs

1½ teaspoons pure vanilla extract

½ cup sour cream

6 ounces (1 cup) bittersweet chocolate chips

1 cup Valrhona crunchy pearls

Preheat the oven to 350°F. Line a 12-cup muffin tin with cupcake papers, and set aside.

In a medium bowl, whisk together the flour, baking powder, and salt, and set aside.

In the bowl of a stand mixer fitted with the paddle attachment, cream the butter and sugar. Blend in the eggs, one at a time, and the vanilla. Add the dry ingredients, in three additions, alternating with the sour cream, and mix just until combined. With a silicone spatula, gently fold in the chocolate chips and crunchy pearls.

Scoop the batter into the cupcake papers. Bake for about 25 minutes, or until the cupcakes begin to brown on the edges and the centers are firm. Remove the cupcakes from the oven, and let cool completely in the tin.

GANACHE FROSTING

12 ounces (2 cups) 70 percent
  bittersweet chocolate, chopped
1 cup heavy cream

Store-bought sugared violets, for
  finishing

Place the chocolate in a large, heat-proof bowl, and set aside.

In a small saucepan, over medium heat, bring the cream to a boil. Pour the hot cream over the chocolate. Stir with a silicone spatula until smooth. Allow the ganache to cool for 10 minutes, then pour it into the bowl of a stand mixer fitted with the whip attachment, and whip for 5 minutes.

Remove the cupcakes from the tin, dollop the frosting onto the cupcakes, and smooth with a small metal offset spatula. Place a sugared violet on top of each, to finish.

CHOCOLATE CHIP—BANANA CAKE WITH PEANUT BUTTER FROSTING

Frederick Aquino of The Standard Grill, High Line

Chef Aquino told me, "I've always loved kick-starting my mornings by eating banana-and-peanut-butter sandwiches with seven-grain bread for breakfast. This recipe is not as healthy as my breakfast, but it has all the flavors that satisfy." For chocolate chip lovers, it is an irresistible wedding cake. • MAKES 16 SERVINGS

BANANA CAKE

¾ pound (3 sticks) unsalted butter, softened, plus more for the pan

4 cups all-purpose flour

1 teaspoon baking powder

1 teaspoon baking soda

1 teaspoon salt

2½ cups granulated sugar

4 large eggs

1 cup sour cream

2 cups mashed bananas (4 medium)

12 ounces (2 cups) bittersweet or semisweet chocolate chips

Preheat the oven to 350°F. Butter three 8-inch round cake pans, line the bottoms with parchment paper, and set aside.

In a medium bowl, combine the flour, baking powder, baking soda, and salt, and set aside.

In the bowl of a stand mixer fitted with the paddle attachment, cream the butter and granulated sugar until light and fluffy. Add the eggs, one at a time, and then the sour cream and bananas. Add the dry ingredients, and mix just until combined. With a silicone spatula, fold in the chocolate chips.

Divide the batter among the prepared pans. Bake for 25 to 30 minutes, until the cakes are firm. Remove from the oven, and let cool completely in the pans.

16 ounces (2 cups) cream cheese, at
room temperature

6 ounces (1½ sticks) unsalted butter,
at room temperature

¼ cup smooth peanut butter

2 cups confectioners' sugar, sifted

½ teaspoon salt

1 teaspoon pure vanilla extract

In the clean bowl of a stand mixer fitted with a clean paddle attachment, mix the cream cheese, butter, and peanut butter together until fluffy. Add the confectioners' sugar, salt, and vanilla, and mix for 1 minute, or until smooth.

Transfer one layer of the cake onto a platter. With an offset spatula, spread the top with a third of the frosting. Place the second layer on top and spread with another third of the frosting. Repeat one more time with the third layer, spreading the remaining frosting evenly on the top and sides of the cake.

LITTLE CHOCOLATE CHIP CHEESECAKES

Tracey Zabar

I originally made this cheesecake as a teenager, but back then I crushed up store-bought, cream-filled chocolate cookies, instead of homemade, for the crust. Now I make mini cheesecakes with chocolate chips inside in little cupcake tins.

• MAKES 48 SMALL CHEESECAKES

4½ tablespoons unsalted butter, melted, plus more, softened, for the tins

18 chocolate chip, chocolate, or amaretti cookies, crushed

⅔ cup plus ¼ cup granulated sugar, divided

16 ounces (2 cups) cream cheese, softened

2 large eggs

1 teaspoon pure vanilla extract

⅔ cup sour cream

6 ounces (1 cup) bittersweet or semisweet chocolate chips

Confectioners' sugar, for dusting (optional)

Edible flowers, for finishing

Preheat the oven to 350°F. Butter two nonstick mini muffin tins, and set aside.

In a medium bowl, mix the crushed cookies, ¼ cup of the granulated sugar, and the melted butter. Sprinkle this mixture on the bottom of each muffin cavity, and set aside.

In the bowl of a stand mixer fitted with the whip attachment, mix the cream cheese and the remaining ⅔ cup granulated sugar. Add the eggs, vanilla, and sour cream, and whisk until fully incorporated. With a silicone spatula, fold in the chocolate chips.

Spoon the batter over the crust in each muffin cavity. Bake for 18 to 20 minutes, until the edges start to brown and the centers are set and start to crack. Remove the cheesecakes from the oven, cool for 10 minutes in the tins, then gently place each cheesecake on a wire rack, and let cool completely. Dust with confectioners' sugar (if using), decorate each with an edible flower, and serve at room temperature or cold. Store leftovers in the refrigerator.

RASPBERRY CHOCOLATE CHUNK SOUFFLÉ

Sherry Yard of Helms Bakery

Sherry Yard, pastry chef extraordinaire, makes many variations of her famous soufflés, but this flavorful raspberry chocolate version is my favorite. It is like eating cotton candy. Yard's legendary soufflé at Spago has been called by many "the best dessert ever." She says, "The almost childish sugary glee of it is the hot pink mousse-y interior, and the melted chocolate in this insane, puffy ode to sugar. This is a dessert with a point of view, but it's the antithesis of the self-serious architectural creations offered by other famous pastry chefs. There's no turning away from the idea that dessert is meant to be fun, that at its heart it's an indulgence and therefore shouldn't become too solemn. This is a celebration of the part of us that, as children, would have risked life and limb—or at least stern punishment—to get our hands on that sweet sticky stuff, and it is the purest expression of that notion (without falling into the trap of mawkish, saccharine overkill) you may ever encounter." · MAKES 8 SOUFFLÉS

RASPBERRY SOUFFLÉ BASE

8 ounces (about 1 cup) raspberries, plus more for garnish

3 tablespoons water

1 tablespoon fresh lemon juice

½ cup granulated sugar

In a stainless steel saucepan, whisk together 1 cup of the raspberries, water, lemon juice, and sugar. Place over a medium flame and stir occasionally until the mixture comes to a boil. Continue whisking, and cook for 4 to 5 more minutes. The raspberry base will now have the consistency of jam. Remove from the heat, pass through a tamis or fine-mesh sieve, and cool to room temperature.

Preheat the oven to 385°F, set on high fan in a convection oven, or 400°F in a traditional oven. Set aside eight 6-ounce ramekins.

¾ cup Raspberry Soufflé Base

8 ounces (1⅓ cups) bittersweet
chocolate, cut into ½-inch pieces

6 large egg whites

¼ teaspoon cream of tartar

½ cup granulated sugar, divided

Raspberries for garnish

In a large stainless steel mixing bowl set over a hot water bath, whisk the raspberry base, and warm it to 60°F. Remove the bowl from the heat, fold in the chocolate chunks, and set aside.

In the bowl of a stand mixer fitted with the whip attachment, whip the egg whites on medium speed until they become foamy, about 1 minute. Add the cream of tartar and 1 tablespoon of the sugar. Continue to whip, adding the remaining sugar slowly in a stream, until the meringue has tripled in size and holds a medium-firm peak. With a balloon whip, fold half of the whipped whites into the raspberry-chocolate base. With a silicone spatula, fold in the remaining egg whites.

Fill a piping bag with the meringue, and cut a super-wide tip. Fill each ramekin to the top, then smooth the top with a palette knife. Run a paring knife around the inside edge of each ramekin. Bake for 8 minutes if you are using a convection setting, or 15 minutes in a traditional oven, until puffed and dark golden. Serve immediately, garnished with raspberries.

VARIATION: Fill seven ramekins to the top, then pipe more meringue on top, for that cotton candy look. You will use more meringue for each, and so you will end up with fewer, taller soufflés.

CHOCOLATE CHIP VICTORIA SPONGE

Jennifer Yee of Lafayette

"This is a simple and handsome cake that is perfect for parties and teatime. The cake itself is great on its own, but the cream filling makes it special," pastry chef Yee writes, "I love the addition of orange flower water in the cream because it adds another dimension to the overall flavor. A little goes a long way." This cake is such a hit in my house that I make it all the time—sometimes with the chocolate chip cream, other times with a ganache poured over the top, and even with whipped cream and berries. · MAKES 12 SERVINGS

LIGHT-AS-AIR CHOCOLATE CHIP SPONGE CAKE

Unsalted butter, softened,
   for the pan

6 large eggs, separated

1¾ cups confectioners' sugar

¼ cup hot water

1 teaspoon pure vanilla extract

Grated zest of 1 orange

1⅓ cups cake flour, sifted

3 ounces (½ cup) mini chocolate
   chips, plus more for sprinkling
   on top

½ teaspoon kosher salt

Preheat the oven to 350°F. Lightly butter the bottom only of a 10-inch spring-form pan (do not butter the sides of the pan) and place a circle of parchment paper in the bottom. Set aside.

In the bowl of a stand mixer fitted with a whip attachment, whisk the egg yolks with the confectioners' sugar on medium-high speed until the mixture is pale and has doubled in volume. Slowly drizzle in the hot water and continue to whisk for another 2 minutes. The mixture should be thick and voluminous. Transfer the mixture to a large bowl, and set aside.

Wash and dry the mixing bowl and whip attachment very well, and reattach the whip attachment. Whisk the egg whites on medium speed until they are thick and foamy, but not grainy. Continue whipping until they hold medium-soft peaks.

While the whites are whisking, move back to the bowl with the yolk mixture. With a silicone spatula, fold in the vanilla and orange zest, then fold in the sifted cake flour, ½ cup of the chocolate chips, and salt. Gently fold in the fluffy egg whites.

Pour the batter into the prepared pan and sprinkle a few additional chips on top. Bake for about 45 minutes, or until the cake is domed and golden, and a toothpick inserted into the center comes out clean. Remove the cake from the oven and allow it to cool completely in the pan. Once the cake is cool, turn the pan on its side and run a sharp knife around the edge of the cake, turning the pan as you go. Place the pan right side up again, and release the spring. Remove the paper from the bottom of the cake.

CHOCOLATE CHIP CREAM

1½ cups heavy cream

2 teaspoons confectioners' sugar, divided

½ teaspoon orange flower water

1½ ounces (¼ cup) mini chocolate chips

Blueberries and blackberries, for finishing

Edible flowers, for finishing

In the bowl of a stand mixer fitted with the whip attachment, whip the cream and 1 teaspoon of the confectioners' sugar together at medium-high speed until firm peaks form. Drizzle in the orange flower water, and whip slowly for a second, just to incorporate. Be careful not to overwhip the cream. With a silicone spatula, gently fold in the chocolate chips.

To assemble the cake: With a serrated knife, cut the sponge cake in half crossways. Place the top half on another plate while you spread the chocolate chip cream over the bottom half. Make sure the cream doesn't go over the edges of the cake. Top the cream with the other cake half. Sift the remaining 1 teaspoon confectioners' sugar over the top before serving. Mound blueberries, blackberries, and edible flowers on top. Serve within the hour, or keep in the refrigerator for up to 4 hours. The cream will start to deflate and weep after that.

SICILIAN PISTACHIO TORTA

Michael White of Marea

Chef White's sweet Italian torta is a showstopper. He combines layers of a simple nut cake with a rich, creamy chocolate chip filling that will have your guests begging for seconds. · MAKES ABOUT 12 SERVINGS

PISTACHIO CAKE

2 tablespoons unsalted butter, melted and cooled to room temperature, plus more, softened, for the pan

6 large eggs

1½ cups granulated sugar

⅔ cup Sicilian pistachios, finely ground, or pistachio flour

⅔ cup cake flour, sifted

Preheat the oven to 325°F. Butter or spray with nonstick cooking spray two 8-inch round cake pans, and set aside.

Place the cooled, melted butter in a medium bowl, and set aside. Combine the eggs and granulated sugar in the bowl of a stand mixer. Place the bowl on top of a double boiler, and heat the eggs and granulated sugar until warm to the touch. Carefully remove the bowl and transfer it to the mixer fitted with the whip attachment. Beat the eggs and sugar until light and fluffy. The mixture should hold a ribbon. Gently fold the ground pistachios and cake flour into the egg mixture. Add a small amount of the batter to the melted butter, then fold it back into the rest of the batter.

Divide the batter between the two prepared pans. Bake for 15 to 20 minutes, until the cakes pull away from the sides of the pans. Remove the cakes from the oven, and cool for 5 minutes, then turn the cakes out onto a wire rack. Let cool completely. If making ahead of time, wrap in plastic wrap and refrigerate.

MASCARPONE FILLING

1½ cups mascarpone, softened

1 cup heavy cream

½ cup confectioners' sugar, plus more
   for dusting

3 ounces (½ cup) mini chocolate chips
   or chopped dark chocolate

When you are ready to assemble and serve the cake, combine the mascarpone, cream, and confectioners' sugar in the clean bowl of a stand mixer fitted with the whip attachment. Whip to stiff peaks. Fold in the chocolate chips.

Trim the cakes so each layer is flat. Place one cake layer on a flat serving plate and top with mascarpone filling. Turn the second cake upside down (so the bottom side of the cake is on top) and sandwich on top of the filling. Dust with sifted confectioners' sugar.

PIES, TARTS,
AND
PASTRIES

STRAWBERRY TARTLETS WITH CHOCOLATE CHIP–RICOTTA FILLING

Nick Malgieri of the Institute of Culinary Education

Any Italian housewife worth her salt has a go-to recipe for *pasta frolla*, which is similar to a shortbread pastry. Nick gave me this one years ago. I have adopted it as my own by adding orange or lemon zest. His strawberry tartlets (*tortine di fragole*) are fresh and delicate, each with a rich ricotta–chocolate chip filling between the crust and the fruit. If you do not have fluted brioche molds, use a miniature cupcake tin. The pastries might not be quite as pretty, but they will be equally delicious. · MAKES 24 TARTLETS

PASTA FROLLA

4 ounces (1 stick) unsalted butter,
   softened
¼ cup granulated sugar
1 teaspoon pure vanilla extract

1 large egg yolk
1¼ cups all-purpose flour (spoon flour
   into a dry-measure cup and level
   off), plus more for rolling

In the bowl of a stand mixer fitted with the paddle attachment, beat the butter, granulated sugar, and vanilla on medium speed until soft and light, about 5 minutes. Beat in the egg yolk, and continue beating until the mixture is soft and smooth. Decrease the speed to low, add the flour, and mix just until combined. Scrape the dough onto a large piece of plastic wrap, and wrap well. Chill the dough for at least 2 hours, or up to 2 days.

When you are ready to bake the tartlets, set a rack in the middle of the oven. Preheat the oven to 350°F. Place twenty-four individual 2½-inch-diameter tartlet pans on a jelly-roll pan.

Remove the dough from the refrigerator and place it on a floured surface. Flour the dough and gently pound it with the rolling pin to soften it. Quickly squeeze and knead the dough together until it is malleable, but still firm and cool. Using about a third of the dough at a time, roll it about ⅛ inch thick, and use a fluted cookie cutter to cut disks of dough, fitting them into the tartlet pans. Before rolling a second piece of dough, incorporate the scraps from the first piece into it. Repeat until all the dough is in the pans. Pierce the crusts all over with a fork.

Bake for 15 to 20 minutes, until the crusts are a light golden color. Remove the jelly-roll pan from the oven, and place on a wire rack. Let the crusts cool completely in the tartlet pans.

CHOCOLATE CHIP–RICOTTA FILLING

1 cup (about ½ pound) whole milk ricotta

¼ cup confectioners' sugar, plus more for dusting

½ teaspoon pure vanilla extract

2 tablespoons mini chocolate chips or chopped chocolate

2 pints strawberries, rinsed, hulled, and drained, for finishing

Whisk the ricotta in a bowl to loosen it, then whisk in ¼ cup of the confectioners' sugar and the vanilla. Fold in the chocolate chips. Cover with plastic wrap and chill in the refrigerator until needed.

To assemble the tartlets: Line up the crusts on a clean jelly-roll pan, and place a spoonful of the filling in each. Top with a strawberry or two, depending on the size, and dust with the reserved confectioners' sugar.

CHOCOLATE CHIP CHERRY COOKIE TART

Pichet Ong

This elegant tart has a distinctive taste, thanks to the combination of chopped bittersweet chocolate and gourmet maraschino cherries. Try to track down the delicious Luxardo brand of cherries (available in a 12.7-ounce jar)—they are soaked in cherry liqueur. For sheer decadence, serve the tart with whipped cream. • MAKES 8 SERVINGS

SHELL

1¼ cups all-purpose flour, plus more
    for rolling

½ cup plus 2 tablespoons Dutch-
    process cocoa powder (preferably
    Valrhona)

⅔ cup granulated sugar

¼ teaspoon Maldon sea salt

5 ounces (1¼ stick) unsalted butter,
    softened

¼ cup ice water

In a food processor, fitted with the metal blade, blend together the flour, cocoa powder, granulated sugar, and Maldon salt until just combined. Add the butter and process until crumbly. Add the ice water and pulse the dough until it comes together. Wrap the dough in plastic wrap, and refrigerate for at least 4 hours until firm.

Place a 9-inch tart pan with a removable bottom on a work surface. Using a rolling pin, roll the dough out until it is about ¼ inch thick and large enough to cover the pan with a slight overhang. Using your fingertips, press the dough evenly onto all sides and the bottom of the pan, removing any extra dough. Prick the bottom of the tart all over with a fork. Refrigerate the pan for 1 hour.

Preheat the oven to 350°F.

Bake the tart shell for 15 minutes. Make the filling while the tart is baking. Remove the shell from the oven, leaving the oven on, and cool completely.

6 ounces (1 cup) white chocolate, chopped

4½ ounces (1 stick plus 1 tablespoon) unsalted butter, cubed

1 vanilla bean, split

1 large egg

1 large egg white

¾ cup packed light brown sugar

1 teaspoon salt

1 teaspoon baking powder

1 cup all-purpose flour

⅓ cup maraschino cherries, drained

4½ ounces (¾ cup) bittersweet chocolate, chopped

¼ teaspoon Maldon sea salt, for finishing

Confectioners' sugar, for dusting

Place the white chocolate in a heat-proof bowl of a stand mixer fitted with the paddle attachment, and set aside.

In a saucepan, cook the butter and vanilla bean over medium heat until the butter turns medium-amber brown, scraping the bottom of the pan occasionally to remove any browned bits. Turn off the heat, remove and discard the vanilla bean. Stir together the brown butter and white chocolate until smooth. Set aside to cool for about 10 minutes. Add the egg and egg white, and combine, then add the brown sugar, salt, and baking powder. Add the flour, and mix just until combined. With a silicone spatula, fold in the cherries, followed by the bittersweet chocolate.

Pour the filling into the pre-baked tart shell.

Bake for 16 to 20 minutes, until golden brown, and the center is set. Remove the tart from the oven, and let cool completely in the pan.

Right before serving, sprinkle on the Maldon salt, and dust the top of the tart with confectioners' sugar. For clean cuts, use a hot knife to slice the tart.

CHOCOLATE CHIP PIE

Tracey Zabar

I often reach for the dog-eared, stained index card with directions for this pie when I am alone in the kitchen with a bag of chocolate chips and no idea how to include them in a dessert. The recipe for this pie filling, titled Darby Pie, has been in our family archives forever. I have forgotten where it came from (perhaps it's a modification of Kentucky Derby Pie, with the pecans and bourbon removed). It is easy to make and most of the ingredients are already in my baking pantry. • MAKES 6 SERVINGS

CRUST

1 cup all-purpose flour

¼ teaspoon salt

3 tablespoons granulated sugar

2 ounces (½ stick) unsalted butter, cubed

1 large egg yolk

1 tablespoon heavy cream

Preheat the oven to 350°F. Place a 9-inch pie pan on a work surface, and set aside.

In the bowl of a stand mixer fitted with the paddle attachment, mix the flour, salt, sugar, butter, egg yolk, and cream, just until a ball forms. Do not overbeat, or the crust will become tough. Pat the dough into the pie pan, and set aside.

FILLING

1 cup granulated sugar

½ cup all-purpose flour

2 ounces (½ stick) unsalted butter, melted and cooled

1 tablespoon pure vanilla extract

6 ounces (1 cup) bittersweet chocolate chips

In a large bowl, with a wooden spoon, toss the sugar, flour, butter, and vanilla just until combined. Fold in the chocolate chips.

Pour the filling into the crust. Bake for 1 hour, or until the edges start to brown. Remove the pie from the oven, and let cool in the pan before serving.

DATE AND CHOCOLATE RUGELACH

Miro Uskokovic of Gramercy Tavern

Chef Uskokovic shared this recipe for rugelach, bursting with chocolate chips. It is quite simple to make, and the results are stunning and delicious. Chocolate and date lovers will be delighted with these ambrosial pastries. · MAKES 12 SERVINGS

2 generous pinches of kosher salt, divided

2¾ cups all-purpose flour

8 ounces (2 sticks) unsalted butter, cut into chunks and kept very cold, plus additional, melted and cooled, for finishing

9 ounces Philadelphia Cream Cheese, cut into chunks and kept very cold

12½ ounces Medjool dates, pitted

⅔ cup fresh orange juice

¼ cup Grand Marnier

8 ounces (1⅓ cups) dark chocolate chips, lightly crushed

Granulated sugar, for finishing

Into a medium bowl, sift together a generous pinch of salt and the flour through a fine-mesh sieve, and set aside.

In the bowl of a stand mixer fitted with the paddle attachment, mix together the 8 ounces of butter and the cream cheese, just until combined, with large chunks still remaining. Add the flour mixture, and mix just enough to combine. Place the dough on a floured surface, and with your hands, bring the dough together. Wrap it in plastic wrap, and place in the refrigerator for at least 1 hour.

While the dough is chilling, make the jam. Combine the dates, orange juice, and the remaining pinch of salt in a small saucepan, and bring to a boil. Turn the temperature down to low heat, and cook for 15 minutes, stirring often. Remove from the heat and cool for about 10 minutes, then process in a food processor, fitted with the metal blade, with the Grand Marnier until it is smooth and has a paste-like consistency. Cool completely.

When the dough is chilled, roll it out on a lightly floured surface to a rect-angle that is about ¼ inch thick. Cut into 5-inch strips. Spread the date jam on top of each strip, and sprinkle with the chocolate chips. Roll each strip the long way into a log, and place it on a half-sheet pan. Chill in the refrigerator for 1 hour, or until firm.

Line two half-sheet pans with parchment paper. Cut the logs into 2-inch slices, and roll each slice in the melted butter, and then in the sugar. Place the slices on the prepared pans, leaving at least 2 inches in between each one. Place the pans in the freezer for at least 30 minutes.

Preheat the oven to 350°F.

Remove the rugelach from the freezer. Bake for 15 to 20 minutes, until golden brown. Remove the rugelach from the oven, transfer to wire racks, and let cool completely.

MRS. PERONI'S PECAN TASSIES

Tracey Zabar

Our friend Mike Peroni's mother once sent us a tin of her famous holiday cookies. These dainty little pastries, similar to pecan pies, were our favorite. I have adapted Mrs. Peroni's recipe by adding chocolate chips. If you don't have tassie cups (tiny tart pans), you can use nonstick muffin tins. Sadly, we lost touch. Mike! Mrs. Peroni! Where are you? • MAKES 30 SMALL SERVINGS

4 ounces (1 stick) unsalted butter, softened, plus 2 ounces (½ stick), melted, divided

5 ounces cream cheese, softened

2 cups all-purpose flour

1 cup chopped pecans

3 tablespoons bittersweet chocolate chips

2 large eggs, beaten

½ cup packed light brown sugar

¼ cup light corn syrup

1 teaspoon pure vanilla bean paste

¼ teaspoon salt

Preheat the oven to 350°F. Place thirty tassie cups on a half-sheet pan that is lined with parchment paper, and set aside.

In the bowl of a stand mixer fitted with the paddle attachment, combine the softened butter and cream cheese. Add the flour, and mix just until combined. Shape into 30 small balls, and press each ball into a tassie cup, forming small pie crusts. With a teaspoon, sprinkle the pecans into the bottom of the each crust. Sprinkle a few chocolate chips into each crust, and set aside. Do not wash the bowl and paddle.

In the same bowl of the stand mixer fitted with the paddle attachment, beat the eggs and brown sugar. Add the corn syrup, melted butter, and vanilla. Add the salt, and mix well. Spoon this mixture into the tassie cups. Bake for about 15 minutes, or until the edges start to brown and the centers are set. Remove the tassies from the oven, and let cool completely in the cups.

SICILIAN CUCIDATI: FIG PASTRIES

Nick Malgieri of the Institute of Culinary Education

Nick says, "These traditional Sicilian Christmas cookies are a bit of a project to make but are worth every minute of it." This filling calls for chopped chocolate instead of chips. • MAKES 60 SMALL PASTRIES

PASTA FROLLA

4 cups all-purpose flour (spoon the
   flour into a dry-measuring cup and
   level off), plus more for rolling
⅔ cup granulated sugar
2 teaspoons baking powder

1 teaspoon salt
8 ounces (2 sticks) unsalted butter,
   cold, and cut into 16 pieces
4 large eggs

Combine the flour, sugar, baking powder, and salt in the bowl of a food processor fitted with the metal blade. Pulse three or four times to mix. Add the butter and pulse repeatedly until it is finely mixed into the dry ingredients. Add the eggs and continue to pulse until the dough forms a ball. Invert the dough onto a floured work surface and carefully remove the blade. Form the dough into a fat cylinder and wrap it in plastic wrap. Chill for 1 hour, or up to 4 days.

FIG FILLING

12-ounce package Calimyrna figs,
   stemmed and diced
¼ cup dark or golden raisins
¼ cup candied orange peel, coarsely
   chopped
¼ cup blanched whole almonds,
   toasted and coarsely chopped
¼ cup pine nuts, toasted
2 ounces (⅓ cup) semisweet chocolate,
   coarsely chopped

¼ cup apricot preserves
¼ cup dark rum
1 teaspoon instant espresso powder
½ teaspoon ground cinnamon
¼ teaspoon ground cloves
Egg wash: 1 large egg, well beaten,
   with a pinch of salt
Multicolored nonpareils, for finishing

In a large bowl, with a silicone spatula, combine the figs, raisins, orange peel, almonds, pine nuts, chopped chocolate, apricot preserves, rum, espresso powder, cinnamon, and cloves.

Scrape the filling into the bowl of a food processor fitted with the metal blade. Pulse repeatedly, until the filling is finely chopped and holds together but is not ground or pureed. Scrape the filling into a bowl and cover it with plastic wrap. Use immediately, or refrigerate for up to 1 week.

To make the pastries: Set racks in the upper and lower thirds of the oven. Preheat the oven to 350°F. Cover three cookie sheets or jelly-roll pans with parchment paper or aluminum foil.

Remove the dough from the refrigerator. Flour a work surface. Gently knead the dough to soften it until malleable. Roll the dough into a cylinder 15 inches long and cut it into fifteen 1-inch slices, and set them aside. Repeat with the filling, adding a bit more flour on the surface.

Clean the work surface and flour it lightly. Roll one of the pieces of dough under the palms of your hands until it is about 8 inches long. Flour under the dough again and use the palm of your hand to flatten it until it is about 3 inches wide. (If you use a rolling pin for this, flour the top of the dough and don't roll over the long edges or it will distort them.) Slide a thin metal spatula under the strip of dough to make sure it isn't stuck.

Flour another part of the work surface, and roll one of the pieces of filling under the palms of your hands until it is 8 inches long. If you do this behind the strip of dough, you can roll it right onto the dough without having to lift it. Center the filling on the dough and lightly brush the egg wash over the exposed edges of dough. Draw the dough around the filling to enclose it and make a long cylinder. Roll the cylinder under the palms of your hands to lengthen it to about 12 inches, being careful not to point the ends while rolling. Use a paring knife to cut the cylinder into four 3-inch lengths. Lightly brush the egg wash over the pastries, and sprinkle with the nonpareils. Arrange the pastries on one of the prepared pans and repeat with the remaining dough and filling.

Bake for 15 to 20 minutes, until the pastries are golden and firm. About halfway through the baking time, switch the pan from the lower rack to the upper one and vice versa, turning the pans back to front at the same time. (If your oven gives strong bottom heat, bake the pan on the lower rack stacked on another pan.) Bake the remaining pan on the middle rack. Remove the pastries from the oven, and let cool on the pans on wire racks.

VARIATION: After you cut the pastries into 3-inch lengths, make 1-inch cuts on one long side of the pastry, and gently pull the slashed areas open.

CHOCOLATE CHIP CANNOLI SANDWICHES

Fortunato Nicotra of Felidia

Chef Nicotra writes, "Cannoli is a traditional Sicilian dessert. To make these pastries, you need special cannoli shell forms around which the dough is rolled and fried. This version has a contemporary, layered look while maintaining a traditional flavor and texture." The inclusion of chocolate chips and candied orange peel in the sweet ricotta filling, with honey and pistachios on top, is glorious. • MAKES 6 TO 9 SERVINGS

1½ cups fresh whole milk ricotta

1½ cups all-purpose flour, plus more for rolling

2 tablespoons granulated sugar

¼ teaspoon salt

2 tablespoons olive oil

1 teaspoon white vinegar

⅓ cup dry red wine, or as needed

¾ cup confectioners' sugar, plus more for dusting

3 tablespoons bittersweet or semisweet chocolate chips

1½ tablespoons finely chopped candied orange peel

1½ tablespoons chopped, toasted pistachios (see Note on page 126), plus more for serving

Vegetable oil, for frying

Honey, for drizzling

Place the ricotta in a cheesecloth-lined sieve and set the sieve over a bowl. Cover the ricotta with plastic wrap and place in the refrigerator for at least 8 hours, or up to 1 day.

Combine the flour, granulated sugar, and salt in a food processor fitted with the metal blade. Add the oil, vinegar, and ⅓ cup of the wine. Process the dough, adding more wine, a few drops at a time if necessary, until the mixture forms a smooth, supple dough. Wrap the dough in plastic wrap and refrigerate for 2 hours, or up to overnight.

Combine the drained ricotta and ¾ cup of the confectioners' sugar in a mixing bowl. Beat with a handheld electric mixer until light and fluffy, about

2 minutes. Fold in the chocolate chips, orange peel, and 1½ tablespoons pistachios. Store in the refrigerator until needed.

On a lightly floured surface, roll half the dough out to ¹⁄₁₆ inch thick, about the thickness of a dime. Cut the dough into 2-inch rounds and transfer the rounds to a lightly floured kitchen towel. Repeat with the other half of the dough. Gather the scraps together and reroll, cutting as many rounds as possible. You will have 12 to 18 rounds. Let the dough rest for at least 15 minutes.

Pour enough of the oil into a large, heavy skillet to fill about ½ inch. Heat over medium heat until the oil appears rippling and an edge of one of the dough rounds gives off a slow sizzle when dipped in the oil. (The oil will register 350°F on a deep-frying thermometer.) Add as many rounds to the oil as will fit without touching. Fry, turning once, until both sides are golden brown, about 2 minutes. The dough circles will bubble and take on an irregular shape as they fry; make sure the oil is deep enough to cook and brown all the surfaces of the dough. Adjust the heat during cooking to maintain a lively sizzle and to give the dough a chance to cook through to the center. Don't allow the oil to get too hot. (The dough colors quickly and can burn before the center is sufficiently cooked.) Transfer the cooked rounds to paper towels to drain and fry the remaining rounds, adding more oil to the pan and waiting for the oil to reheat as necessary. Cool the circles completely before continuing.

Place a circle of the fried dough in the center of a serving plate and top with a rounded 2 tablespoons of the ricotta filling. Top with another dough circle. Repeat with the remaining ingredients to make a total of 6 to 9 cannoli sandwiches. Drizzle honey over each and dust with confectioners' sugar. Sprinkle some of the remaining chopped, toasted pistachios around each cannoli.

NOTE: To make chopped, toasted pistachios, first shell the nuts. Blanch the shelled nuts in vigorously boiling unsalted water until they turn bright green and the skins are loosened, about 20 seconds. Drain the nuts and immediately run them under cold water. Slip off the skins and drain the nuts briefly on paper towels. Toast on a baking sheet in a 350°F oven until lightly browned, about 10 minutes. Cool completely before chopping.

BUTTERSCOTCH CHOCOLATE CHIP ÉCLAIRS

Jennifer Yee of Lafayette

"We take great pride in our éclairs at Lafayette," pastry chef Yee says. "We take equal pride in our chocolate chip cookies, which have lots of brown sugar and coffee extract for full-on flavor. This recipe is what you'd get if they had a baby." And what sweet little babies, indeed. · MAKES 12 ÉCLAIRS

BUTTERSCOTCH PUDDING

1 cup packed dark brown sugar

½ teaspoon kosher salt

1½ cups water

2 cups heavy cream

1 cup whole milk

4 large egg yolks

1½ tablespoons cornstarch

1 teaspoon dark rum

3 tablespoons unsalted butter, cubed

In a medium saucepan, cook the brown sugar, salt, and water over medium heat for about 10 minutes, or until smoky and the mixture reduces down to a sticky caramel paste, constantly stirring with a wooden spoon to prevent scorching.

In another medium saucepan, heat the cream and milk to a scald. Once the caramel is done, turn off the heat under it and slowly and carefully add the milk mixture, stirring at the same time. Return to the heat. Bring to a boil, and turn off the heat.

In a medium bowl, whisk together the egg yolks and cornstarch until combined. Pour about a cup of the hot liquid into the egg mixture, and whisk vigorously to prevent the eggs from curdling. Whisk in another cup of liquid. Now pour this hot egg mixture back into the pan, and cook on medium heat, whisking constantly, until the mixture thickens slightly. This will take about another 5 minutes. Remove from the heat, carefully add the rum and butter, and whisk until fully incorporated.

Transfer the pudding to a medium heat-proof bowl to cool. Lay a sheet of plastic wrap right on the surface of the pudding to prevent a skin from forming.

Place the pudding in the refrigerator to cool completely, for at least 4 hours or preferably overnight.

PÂTE À CHOUX

⅓ cup water

⅓ cup milk, preferably skim or
2 percent

2 ounces (½ stick) unsalted butter, cut into ½-inch cubes

¾ teaspoon granulated sugar

¼ teaspoon salt

1½ cups all-purpose flour

3 large eggs

In a medium saucepan, bring the water, milk, butter, sugar, and salt to a boil. Turn off the heat, and immediately dump all the flour into the pan at once. Stir with a wooden spoon until the mixture is homogenous. Now turn the heat on to medium, and continue cooking and stirring until a thin film of dough sticks to the bottom of the pan, about 5 minutes.

Transfer the hot batter into the bowl of a stand mixer fitted with the paddle attachment. Mix on medium-low speed for about 2 minutes to allow the batter to cool down a bit before you add the eggs. Drop the eggs into the moving batter, one at a time, scraping the bowl between each addition. This batter should have a silky paste consistency. Cover the bowl with plastic wrap right on the surface, and chill for about 1 hour.

Preheat the oven to 375°F. Line two half-sheet pans with parchment paper.

Place the batter in a pastry bag fitted with a large French star tip (such as Ateco #879). Pipe 5-inch-long tubes of batter onto the prepared pans, about 3 inches apart. Lightly mist the piped éclairs with a water sprayer. This keeps the batter moist and prevents too much cracking in the oven.

Bake for 30 to 40 minutes, until golden all over. Please don't be tempted to open the oven door until the éclairs have at least gotten a good amount of color, as this will allow the steam in the oven to escape, which may deflate them. Once they are baked and golden, turn off the oven, and let cool completely in the oven with the door open, to allow the interior of the éclairs to dry out and allow for more filling.

CHOCOLATE CHIP TOPPING

6 ounces (1 cup) mini chocolate chips

5 ounces (1 cup) fondant icing (also known as pouring fondant, not rolled fondant)

½ to 1½ teaspoons warm water, as needed

½ teaspoon coffee extract

Place the chocolate chips in a shallow bowl, and set aside.

In a heat-proof bowl, combine the fondant icing, water, and coffee extract, and mix until combined. Place the bowl over a saucepan of lightly simmering water and stir constantly until the mixture reaches 95°F. (Keep the saucepan on the stove, in case the glaze needs to be rewarmed before you use it.) Use the glaze immediately.

Punch 3 small holes in the bottom of each éclair using a small star pastry tip or the end of a clean pair of scissors. Place the butterscotch pudding in a pastry bag, and snip a small opening in the end. Pipe the pudding into the holes until it starts to ooze out a little. The filled éclairs should feel heavy for their size.

Dip the top third of each éclair into the coffee glaze and sweep off any excess glaze with an index finger. (If the glaze cools too much while dipping, place the bowl over simmering water to warm it up again.) If the glaze is too thick to dip, stir in more water, ½ teaspoon at a time, as needed. Gently press the éclair, glaze side down, into the chocolate chips. Place on a tray, chips side up. Repeat with each of the remaining éclairs, and allow the glaze to set for about 10 minutes before serving. Refrigerate the éclairs if you are not serving them immediately.

CHAPTER

№ **6**

SPOON DESSERTS

AND

HOT DRINKS

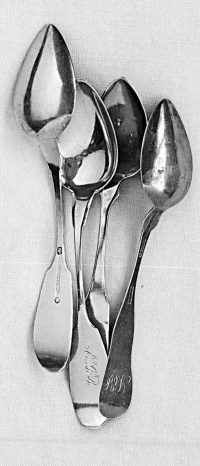

CHOCOLATE CHIP PAVLOVAS FOR ICE-CREAM SUNDAES

Nicole Kaplan of Rôtisserie Georgette

According to legend, the pavlova, a meringue dessert, was created in honor of the great Russian ballerina Anna Pavlova. Making pavlovas with chocolate chips as the base of ice-cream sundaes brings this almost hundred-year-old dessert to a whole new level. Prepare pastry chef Kaplan's dreamy dessert over a two-day period. Start with the whipped cream, hot fudge, and ice cream the day before so that they can set up in the refrigerator or freezer. Make the meringue shells, which become the base of the sundaes, and the streusel the day you plan to serve them. · MAKES 5 SUNDAES

MILK CHOCOLATE WHIPPED CREAM

3 ounces (½ cup) milk chocolate, chopped

2 cups heavy cream, divided

Place the chocolate in a medium, heat-proof bowl. In a small saucepan, bring 1 cup of the cream to a boil. Pour the hot cream over the chocolate, and whisk until fully melted. Add in the remaining 1 cup cream.

Let cool, cover the bowl with plastic wrap, and place in the refrigerator overnight. The cream will not whip properly unless it has had a chance to fully cool overnight. When you are ready to serve, place the cream in the bowl of a stand mixer fitted with the whip attachment, and whip to soft peaks.

MILK CHOCOLATE ICE CREAM

12 ounces (2 cups) milk chocolate, chopped

1 cup granulated sugar, divided

10 egg yolks

1 quart milk

2 cups heavy cream

If your ice-cream maker has a removable bowl that needs to freeze overnight, place it in the freezer the night before you make the ice cream.

Fill a large bowl with ice, and set aside.

In a large, heat-proof bowl, place the chocolate, and set aside.

In a medium, heat-proof bowl, place ½ cup of the granulated sugar and the egg yolks, whisk together, and set aside.

In a medium saucepan, bring the milk, cream, and the remaining ½ cup granulated sugar to a boil. Temper (so that your yolks don't scramble) by pouring a small amount of the hot milk mixture into the yolks, then add a bit more, whisking constantly. Pour the yolks into the milk, and gently continue to whisk for an additional minute to just slightly thicken the mixture. Strain this mixture over the chocolate, and whisk to fully melt. Cool in the ice bath, cover the mixture with plastic wrap, and let sit overnight in the refrigerator.

Process in an ice-cream machine according to the manufacturer's directions, and freeze.

HOT FUDGE

1 cup whole milk	2½ tablespoons unsalted butter, cubed
1 cup heavy cream	12 ounces (2 cups) semisweet
⅓ cup granulated sugar	chocolate, chopped

In a medium saucepan, bring the milk, cream, and granulated sugar to a boil. Whisk in the butter and chocolate, and continue cooking until you have reached a boil again, whisking continuously to avoid burning the chocolate. Pour into a container, cover with plastic wrap, and let cool in the refrigerator.

CHOCOLATE STREUSEL

1 cup all-purpose flour	½ teaspoon salt
3 tablespoons cornstarch	⅔ cup granulated sugar
5 tablespoons Dutch-process cocoa	12 tablespoons (1½ sticks) unsalted
powder	butter, cut into ¼-inch cubes
¾ cup almond flour	

Preheat the oven to 350°F. Line a half-sheet pan with parchment paper; set aside.

In the bowl of a stand mixer fitted with the paddle attachment, mix the flour, cornstarch, cocoa powder, almond flour, salt, granulated sugar, and butter together until nice, evenly sized crumbs form.

Scrape the mixture onto the prepared pan, and bake in the oven for about 15 minutes, or until it is toasty and dried out a bit. Check to make sure that the streusel doesn't burn. Remove the streusel from the oven, and cool completely on the pan.

MERINGUE SHELLS

4 large egg whites

Pinch of salt

1 cup granulated sugar

3 ounces (½ cup) bittersweet or semisweet chocolate chips

Confectioners' sugar, for sprinkling

Preheat the oven to 200°F. With a pencil or marker, trace five 4-inch circles on a piece of parchment paper, flip the paper over, line a half-sheet pan with the parchment, and set aside.

In the clean bowl of a stand mixer fitted with a clean whip attachment, whip the egg whites and salt to soft peaks. Slowly add the granulated sugar, 1 tablespoon at a time, and whip until it is soft, billowy, and the consistency of shaving cream. With a silicone spatula, gently fold in the chocolate chips.

Pipe or spoon the meringue onto the prepared pans, using the circles as your guide, making 4-inch-wide mounds that are nice and full. Sprinkle the tops with some sifted confectioners' sugar. Bake for 1 to 2 hours (depending on your oven), or until the outsides are dry and crisp but the centers are still slightly soft and the consistency of a marshmallow. Remove the meringues from the oven, and let cool completely on the pans.

When you are ready to serve: Place a meringue shell on a plate. Place 2 small scoops of ice cream in the center. Dollop a mound of the chocolate whipped cream on top, and add a sprinkle of streusel. Pour some hot fudge on top.

NOTE: You can make the shells any size you want. Just trace larger or smaller circles on your parchment paper, and keep an eye on the meringues in the oven, because the baking time will change.

MINT CHOCOLATE CHIP ICE CREAM

Shaun Hergatt of Juni

There is ice cream with mint chips and mint ice cream with chocolate chips. Chef Hergatt's sweet and refreshing treat is the latter. He says, "I lived for chocolate chip and mint ice cream as a child. It was one of those memories that never faded—I still relish in the joy of that specific texture and classic flavor profile." I recently tried his recipe with spearmint oil, as that was all I had in the kitchen. A visiting child declared it to be "the best chewing-gum ice cream ever." But I highly recommend that you use peppermint oil instead. · MAKES 1 QUART

2 cups whole milk

1½ cups heavy cream

½ cup large egg yolks (about 6)

1 cup granulated sugar

½ teaspoon salt

3 tablespoons mint oil, such as
  peppermint oil

4½ ounces (¾ cup) bittersweet
  chocolate chips

If your ice-cream maker has a removable bowl that needs to freeze overnight, place it in the freezer the night before you make the ice cream.

Fill a large bowl with ice, and place it next to your stove.

In a medium saucepan, combine the milk, cream, egg yolks, sugar, salt, and mint oil. Emulsify the ingredients with an immersion blender. (If you do not have an immersion blender, mix the ingredients in the bowl of a stand mixer fitted with the whip attachment, or in a food processor, fitted with the metal blade, then pour the mixture into the saucepan.) Place the saucepan on your stove top, and gently heat the mixture to 180°F. Remove the pan from the heat, and place it in the ice bath until it is cool. Pour the mixture into a container, cover with plastic wrap, and place in the refrigerator overnight.

The next day, spin the ice cream in an ice-cream maker, according to the manufacturer's directions. When the ice cream is frozen, fold in the chocolate chips. Place the ice cream in a container, covered, in the freezer.

MARSHMALLOW CHOCOLATE CHIP COOKIE DOUGH ICE CREAM

Florian Bellanger of Mad Mac

Unbaked cookie dough is an enticing indulgence, but a dangerous one if you are consuming raw eggs. Pastry chef Bellanger solved this issue by eliminating the eggs from this recipe, which is packed with marshmallows and two kinds of chocolate chips. · MAKES ABOUT 24 SERVINGS

5⅓ tablespoons (⅓ cup) unsalted
   butter, softened
⅓ cup packed light brown sugar
¼ cup granulated sugar
1 teaspoon pure vanilla extract
2 tablespoons light corn syrup
1 cup plus 1 tablespoon all-purpose
   flour

Pinch of salt
2 ounces (⅓ cup) dark chocolate chips
2 cups mini marshmallows
3 ounces (½ cup) mini chocolate chips
3 pints vanilla ice cream, preferably
   Häagen-Dazs

In the bowl of a stand mixer fitted with the paddle attachment, cream the butter, brown sugar, and granulated sugar. Add the vanilla and corn syrup. Sift in the flour and salt, and mix. With a silicone spatula, fold in the dark chocolate chips. Cover the bowl with plastic wrap and refrigerate for 1 hour.

Place the marshmallows and mini chocolate chips in a small bowl. Cover with plastic wrap, and refrigerate for 1 hour.

Remove the cookie dough from the refrigerator and break into bite-size pieces. Remove the marshmallows and mini chips from the refrigerator.

Transfer the vanilla ice cream to a very clean bowl of a stand mixer, and place the empty ice-cream containers on your work surface. Using a clean paddle attachment, on low speed, soften the ice cream. You do not want it to get too soft or melted. Add the cookie dough pieces, marshmallows, and mini chips. Mix just a few seconds until combined, refill the ice-cream containers, and freeze immediately.

PER SE BUTTER CARAMEL

Thomas Keller and Elwyn Boyles of Per Se

Chef Keller and Chef Boyles use this French confection, a light, buttery caramel, as a spread on a fresh baguette or toast; added to peanut butter; mixed with yogurt and granola for a sweet breakfast; spread on cake; between thin short-bread cookies to create a cookie caramel sandwich; as a filling in a pie, such as a banoffee; or as a rich caramel sauce ladled over my favorite, chocolate chip ice cream. • MAKES 5 CUPS

4½ cups heavy cream
½ cup glucose syrup or light corn
   syrup

2 teaspoons fleur de sel
1 cup granulated sugar
⅓ cup plus 2 teaspoons unsalted butter

Sanitize canning jars by running them through the dishwasher and then dipping them in boiling water for at least 20 seconds. Dry and set aside.

In a medium saucepan over a medium-high heat, bring the cream, glucose syrup, and fleur de sel to a simmer, whisking so the salt does not settle to the bottom and burn. Remove from the heat and set aside.

In a large saucepan set on medium heat, make a dry caramel with the sugar by adding it in stages to the pan until there are no more sugar crystals present and you have a nice amber caramel. Remove from the heat.

Gradually deglaze the sugar by slowly adding the cream mixture into the sugar. Be careful, because this will bubble up and put off very hot steam. Place the pan over medium-high heat, whisk, and cook until the mixture reaches 221°F. Remove from the heat and allow it to cool for 10 to 15 minutes. Transfer the caramel to a blender, add the butter, and blend until fully emulsified.

Transfer the caramel to the prepared canning jars and loosely apply the lids. Place the jars in a large pot of room-temperature water. Place on the stove and, over high heat, bring to a boil. Once the water boils, shut the heat off. Set a timer for 20 minutes and then carefully remove the jars from the water. Check to make sure that the lids are sealed. Cool to room temperature.

COCONUT CHOCOLATE CHIP ICE-CREAM SANDWICHES

Pichet Ong

Pichet Ong created this cookie recipe when he was the pastry chef at New York City's Spice Market restaurant. The surprising addition of toasted coconut to a perfect, classic chocolate chip dough gives the cookies a distinctive taste and texture. Make ice-cream sandwiches using vanilla bean (or any flavor you prefer) ice cream. • MAKES ABOUT 18 ICE-CREAM SANDWICHES

1⅓ cups unsweetened finely shredded coconut

2 cups all-purpose flour

1½ teaspoons baking powder

8 ounces (2 sticks) unsalted butter, softened

¾ cup plus 1 tablespoon granulated sugar

1 cup packed dark brown sugar

½ teaspoon salt

2 large eggs

2 teaspoons pure vanilla extract

18 ounces (3 cups) chocolate chips or pistoles (66 percent to 72 percent chocolate), roughly chopped

2 pints vanilla bean ice cream

Preheat the oven to 300°F. Line a half-sheet pan with parchment paper.

Spread the coconut on the prepared pan. Bake for about 7 minutes, or until golden brown and fragrant. Turn the oven off, remove the pan from the oven, and set it aside to cool completely.

In a medium bowl, sift together the flour and baking powder, and set aside.

In the bowl of a stand mixer fitted with the paddle attachment, combine the butter, granulated sugar, brown sugar, salt, and cooled toasted coconut into the bowl of a stand mixer fitted with the paddle attachment. Mix on medium speed for 3 minutes, until light and fluffy. With the machine running, add the eggs, one at a time, and the vanilla. Turn the mixer speed to low and add half of the dry ingredients. When incorporated, add the remaining dry ingredients, and mix just until no traces of flour remain. Fold in the chocolate chips. Cover with plastic wrap, and chill for at least 2 hours or up to 3 days before baking.

Preheat the oven to 325°F. Line two half-sheet pans with parchment paper, and set aside.

Scoop the cookie dough into 1-inch balls and place them 2 inches apart on the prepared pans. Bake for about 12 minutes, or until brown and crisp. Remove the cookies from the oven, and let cool completely on the pans on wire racks.

Place the cookies, flat side up, on your work surface. Spread slightly softened ice cream on half of the cookies. Place the remaining cookies on top, flat side down, to create sandwiches, and return them to one of the parchment-lined pans. Wrap the entire tray with plastic wrap and freeze until set, at least 6 hours, preferably overnight.

DOUBLE CHOCOLATE CHUNK BREAD PUDDING WITH WARM CARAMEL SAUCE

Micol Negrin of Rustico Cooking

Chef Negrin told me, "The inspiration for this simple, homey pudding came when I had way too much panettone left after Christmas. In Lombardy, where I grew up, they bake lovely cakes with leftover panettone, Marsala, and eggs after the holidays are over. So I played with the recipe a bit, added orange zest (that's the secret ingredient here, and it makes all the difference) and chocolate chunks. I prefer the bread pudding slightly warm." · MAKES 7 SERVINGS

CUSTARD

Nonstick cooking spray

3 large eggs

½ cup granulated sugar, divided

Grated zest of ½ large orange

1 tablespoon rum or sweet Marsala

⅔ cup whole milk

⅔ cup heavy cream

10 ounces brioche, panettone, or pound cake, cut into ½-inch cubes

2 ounces (¼ cup) bittersweet chocolate, coarsely chopped

2 ounces (¼ cup) white chocolate, coarsely chopped

Preheat the oven to 375°F (preferably set on convection bake). Spray seven individual ramekins (½-cup capacity) with nonstick cooking spray. Place the ramekins on a parchment paper–lined baking sheet, and set aside.

In a large bowl, beat the eggs with all but 1 tablespoon of the granulated sugar, the orange zest, and the rum. Add the milk and cream, beat again, and set aside.

Divide the brioche, bittersweet chocolate, and white chocolate among the prepared ramekins. Pour the custard evenly over the brioche and chocolate. Gently push with the tips of your fingers so that the brioche sinks into the custard. The chocolate should be hidden under the brioche or it may burn in the oven. Sprinkle the tops with the remaining 1 tablespoon of granulated sugar.

Bake for about 22 minutes, or until set and golden. The sides should shrink slightly from the ramekins when the puddings are fully cooled and the middle should no longer be jiggly. Let rest for 15 minutes, then unmold. Serve the puddings warm or at room temperature with a touch of caramel sauce and a tuft of whipped cream.

CARAMEL SAUCE

1 tablespoon unsalted butter

⅓ cup plus 1 tablespoon packed light
    brown sugar

⅓ cup plus 1 tablespoon heavy cream

1 teaspoon honey

1 teaspoon rum

1 teaspoon cornstarch dissolved in
    1 teaspoon cool water (optional)

In a small saucepan, combine the butter, brown sugar, cream, honey, and rum, and cook over medium heat, whisking, until smooth and melted, about 2 minutes. Bring to a boil, still whisking. Cook, whisking often, over low heat, until the sauce reduces by half, about 20 minutes. Watch that the sauce does not burn. It must be kept on a very low heat. If you would like a thicker sauce, return to a boil, stir in the cornstarch mixture, and cook until the sauce is thick, whisking all the while to avoid lumps. Remove from the heat, and set aside.

WHIPPED CREAM

½ cup heavy cream

1 tablespoon confectioners' sugar

½ teaspoon pure vanilla extract

With a balloon whisk, whip the cream to soft peaks in a chilled bowl. Whisk in the confectioners' sugar and vanilla.

CHOCOLATE POT-DE-CRÈME WITH SALTED PEANUT CRUMBLE

Matthew Neele of Wallsé

Pastry chef Neele's chocolate pot-de-crème is one of the best puddings I have ever eaten. He says, "This little cup of goodness can really put life into perspective. Also chocolate, salt, and peanuts are a classic combination that shouldn't ever be questioned. I have made this many a time in my career and will easily say that sitting in the walk-in at 1:00 a.m., eating this, is better than ice cream after a horrid day." · MAKES 20 SERVINGS

CHOCOLATE PUDDING

7½ ounces (1¼ cups) dark chocolate, such as Valrhona Manjari, coarsely chopped

3 cups heavy cream

¼ cup granulated sugar

1 vanilla bean

10 large egg yolks

5 large eggs

Place twenty small coffee cups or mini parfait glasses on your work surface.

In a heat-proof bowl of a stand mixer fitted with the whip attachment, place the chocolate, and set aside.

In a medium saucepan, combine the cream and sugar. With a small paring knife, split the vanilla bean lengthwise and scrape the seeds into the pan. Add the bean, and simmer.

In a medium bowl, mix the egg yolks and eggs until combined. Now slowly add the egg mixture to the simmering cream, and stir continuously, making sure not to curdle the eggs. Remove and discard the vanilla bean. Once the cream thickens, pour it over the reserved chocolate, and whisk at low speed until light and fluffy.

Pour the pudding into the prepared coffee cups or mini parfait glasses, and place in the refrigerator for 3 to 4 hours, until firm.

SALTED PEANUT CRUMBLE

4 ounces (1 stick) unsalted butter

1 cup milk solids (powdered milk)

1 cup crushed peanuts

1 tablespoon Maldon sea salt

Bittersweet or semisweet chocolate
chips or curls, for garnish

Preheat the oven to 325°F. Line a half-sheet pan with a piece of parchment paper, and set aside.

In a small, deep saucepan, melt the butter. Add the milk solids, and stir until combined and golden brown.

Scrape the mixture onto the prepared pan. Bake for 10 minutes. Remove the crumble from the oven, and let cool completely on the pan. Add in the peanuts and salt. Spoon a bit of this crumble on top of each pudding, and garnish with chocolate chips. Now grab a spoon and put your phone on silent.

CHOCOLATE CHIP PUDDING

Jonathan Waxman of Barbuto

Chef Waxman's pudding is simple to make and astoundingly sweet and delicious. The addition of chocolate chips transforms this rich dessert into comfort food. · MAKES 6 SERVINGS

3 ounces (¾ stick) unsalted butter,
   plus more for the pans
1¼ cups heavy cream
3 egg yolks
1 tablespoon granulated sugar

⅓ teaspoon salt
8 ounces (1⅓ cups) bittersweet or
   semisweet chocolate chips
1 teaspoon pure vanilla extract

Preheat the oven to 250°F. Butter six 4-ounce ramekins. Place them in a large baking pan, and set aside.

In the bowl of a stand mixer fitted with the whip attachment, whisk the cream, egg yolks, sugar, and salt together for 2 minutes.

Place the chocolate chips in a heat-proof stainless steel bowl, add the vanilla, and set aside.

Heat 3 ounces of the butter until sizzling, and pour over the chips. When the chips are soft, stir and add the yolk mixture, mixing carefully.

Pour the pudding into the prepared ramekins, and place the baking pan filled with the ramekins in the oven. Prepare a bain-marie by carefully pouring very hot water into the baking pan, making sure not to splash any water into the puddings. Bake for 30 minutes, or until set. Remove the puddings from the oven, and let cool in the ramekins. Serve warm or at room temperature.

HOT CHOCOLATE, THREE WAYS

Tracey Zabar

This European-style drink is thick and very chocolaty. If you choose to serve it hot, float one of Chef Acosta and Chef Iuzzini's marshmallows (see page 148) on top. • MAKES 4 SERVINGS

6 ounces Valrhona Guanaja
  70 percent dark chocolate
1 cup heavy cream
1 cup whole milk

4 marshmallows
Bittersweet or semisweet chocolate
  chips, for finishing

Place 4 coffee cups next to your work surface.

Chop the chocolate in a food processor, fitted with the metal blade. Place in a large, heat-proof bowl, and set aside.

In a small saucepan, bring the cream and milk to a boil. Pour the hot cream mixture over the chocolate, and whisk until smooth. Strain through a fine-mesh sieve into another heat-proof bowl and ladle into the coffee cups. Immediately float a marshmallow and a few chocolate chips on top, and serve hot.

ICED HOT CHOCOLATE

After you strain the hot chocolate into the heat-proof bowl, let it cool for 20 minutes. Fill four tall glasses with ice, stir the hot chocolate, and pour over the ice.

ICED MOCHA

Make a pot of hazelnut coffee. Add milk and sugar to the pot, and cool to room temperature. Stir, pour into ice-cube trays, and freeze. Make Iced Hot Chocolate, as above, and substitute the frozen coffee cubes for the ice. As the cubes melt, the chocolate flavor turns into mocha.

CHOCOLATE CHIP MARSHMALLOWS

Alina Martell Acosta of Ai Fiori

Pastry chef Acosta writes, "This recipe is based on the beautiful marshmallows at Jean-Georges. There were always three flavors, stacked on top of one another, in a glass jar, that were served to guests at the end of the meal. In my time there with pastry chef Johnny Iuzzini, there was a whole range of flavors we tried. While I never remember folding in any chocolate chips or bits of chocolate, the recipe, modified a bit, works so well with almost anything."

• MAKES 16 MARSHMALLOWS

Nonstick cooking spray

5 sheets leaf gelatin (silver strength)

Ice water, as needed

4 large egg whites, at room temperature

1 cup granulated sugar

2 tablespoons glucose syrup or corn syrup

Water, as needed

4½ ounces (¾ cup) mini chocolate chips or 70 percent chocolate, finely chopped

Confectioners' sugar, for dusting

Cornstarch, for dusting

Line an 8-inch square baking pan with plastic wrap. Lightly spray with nonstick cooking spray, and set aside.

Bloom, or soak, the gelatin sheets in a bowl of ice water for 10 minutes, and set aside.

In a heat-proof bowl of a stand mixer fitted with the whip attachment, whisk the egg whites on low speed, and set aside.

In a small saucepan, combine the granulated sugar and glucose syrup with just enough water to cover. Cook the sugar mixture until it measures 310°F on a candy thermometer. Remove from the heat.

With your hands, remove the bloomed gelatin from the water, squeeze out the excess liquid, and stir into the sugar mixture.

Turn the mixer up to high speed and slowly stream the cooked sugar into the whipping egg whites, making sure to pour the sugar onto the inside of the bowl to avoid getting the hot liquid on the whip. Continue to whip until the marshmallow cools, and is just slightly warm to the touch. Fold in the chocolate chips, and spread into the prepared pan. Let the marshmallow set for at least an hour. Flip the marshmallow out onto a second piece of plastic wrap, sprayed with nonstick cooking spray.

Wrap the marshmallow, and allow it to set up overnight, at room temperature. Unwrap, and lightly dust both sides of the marshmallow with a mixture of equal parts confectioners' sugar and cornstarch. Cut with a sharp knife, sprayed with the nonstick spray, into 2-inch squares.

BETONY HOT CHOCOLATE

Eamon Rockey and Bryce Shuman of Betony

This hot chocolate is one of the few recipes that I allowed into the book even though it directs you to melt the chocolate, and so technically there are no chips or chunks in it. It's so good that I don't care. The subtle taste of honey and molasses brings this classic winter drink to a whole new level. Since the truffle paste is a very sophisticated addition, I took the liberty of making it optional. · MAKES 20 SERVINGS

6 ounces (1 cup) Valrhona 70 percent
   chocolate, chopped
1 tablespoon honey
1 tablespoon molasses
Pinch of kosher salt

½ vanilla bean
½ cup whole milk, heated, for each
   serving
1 teaspoon black truffle paste
   (optional)

Line a half-sheet pan with parchment paper or food-safe acetate, and set aside.

In the top of a double boiler, over medium heat, combine the chocolate, honey, molasses, and salt. With the tip of a sharp paring knife, scrape the seeds of the vanilla bean, add them to the mixture, and slowly melt the chocolate on medium heat. Blend, using an immersion blender, or transfer the mixture to a food processor, fitted with the metal blade, and blend until smooth. With a silicone spatula, scrape the mixture onto the prepared pan, and let it set at room temperature. Cut this base into 20 portions.

When you are ready to serve, melt one portion of the hot chocolate base in the hot milk (an espresso wand works quite well, or use a small saucepan over medium heat). Once combined, add the truffle paste (if using). Stir and serve.

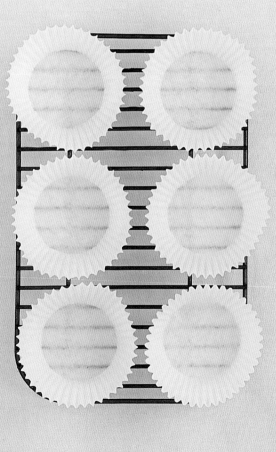

CHOCOLATE CHIP CEREAL BARS

Pichet Ong

Pastry chef Ong made these amazing cereal bars for me to taste. Then he gave me the recipe, and it looked like there were certainly typos. Thirteen cups of marshmallows and 16 cups of cereal couldn't possibly fit in one pan, along with all the other ingredients, but they miraculously did indeed. The addition of white chocolate and almonds was a delightful surprise in this classic lunch box standard. Sometimes pastry chef Ong uses other types of nuts, such as pecans or peanuts, and he always uses the best-quality chocolate. For an interesting variation, he adds chopped-up candies, such as Skor, Maltesers, or Reese's Peanut Butter Cups. · MAKES ABOUT 16 SERVINGS

4 ounces (1 stick) unsalted butter

13 cups marshmallows

1 teaspoon salt

4½ ounces (¾ cup) white chocolate, coarsely chopped

¾ cup almonds, skin on, toasted and chopped

16 cups rice cereal

12 ounces (2 cups) chopped bittersweet chocolate

Line a half-sheet pan with a piece of parchment paper that is slightly larger than the pan, and set aside.

In a large saucepan, heat the butter, marshmallows, and salt over medium-low heat until melted. Be very careful not to let the mixture burn. Fold in the white chocolate, and allow it to melt. Remove the pan from the heat, stir in the almonds, and add the cereal. With a silicone spatula, working quickly, fold the mixture until the marshmallow coats the cereal, and all the ingredients are incorporated. Fold in the bittersweet chocolate, and quickly transfer the mixture to the prepared pan. Press gently with a spatula to pack down the cereal. The cereal bars will be about 2 inches higher than the edge of the pan. Set aside to cool completely in the pan. Invert the pan onto a clean cutting board. Using a large, very sharp knife, cut into 16 rectangular bars.

GRANOLA SQUARES WITH CHOCOLATE CHIPS

Tracey Zabar

My granola squares are sticky, super sweet, and packed with dried fruit, honey, and, of course, chocolate chips. · MAKES 16 SQUARES

2 cups old-fashioned rolled oats
  (not instant)
1½ cups dried fruit (a combination
  of raisins, cherries, blueberries,
  and figs)
½ cup sliced almonds
½ cup unsweetened shredded coconut
4 ounces (1 stick) unsalted butter,
  melted

½ cup honey
½ cup packed light brown sugar
½ teaspoon pure vanilla extract
½ teaspoon salt
3 ounces (½ cup) Valrhona chocolate
  pearls
3 ounces (½ cup) mini chocolate chips

Preheat the oven to 350°F. Line an 8-inch square baking pan with parchment paper that is slightly larger than the pan, and set aside.

In a large bowl, using a wooden spoon, combine the oats, fruit, almonds, coconut, butter, honey, brown sugar, vanilla, salt, chocolate pearls, and chocolate chips. The mixture will be sticky.

Scrape the mixture into the prepared pan. Bake for 20 to 25 minutes, until the edges start to brown. Remove the granola from the oven and cool completely in the pan. Cover the pan with plastic wrap and place in the refrigerator overnight. Remove from the refrigerator and lift the entire parchment, with the granola, out of the pan. Cut into 2-inch squares.

GRANDMA JULIA'S BANANA BREAD
Randie Malinsky

My friend Randie gave me her Grandma Julia Waldbaum's wonderful banana bread recipe twenty years ago, and she never minded that I threw in some chocolate chips. Though most people eat banana bread for breakfast, her family always enjoyed it as a dessert with whipped cream, accompanied by coffee. When Randie made her grandmother's bread, she recalled Julia's Brooklyn kitchen. Just like Julia, the family makes her signature bread entirely by hand, and bakes it in a special tall and narrow Bundt pan. It doesn't matter what shape pan you use, your kitchen will smell yummy and the cake will be delicious.

• MAKES ABOUT 12 SERVINGS

4 ounces (1 stick) sweet butter, softened, plus more for the pan

1½ cups all-purpose flour, plus more for the pan

1½ cups granulated sugar

2 large eggs

1 teaspoon baking soda

Pinch of salt

4 heaping tablespoons sour cream

3 ripe bananas, mashed

3 ounces (½ cup) bittersweet chocolate chips

Preheat the oven to 350°F. Butter and flour a Bundt pan or two loaf pans, and set aside.

In a large bowl, with a wooden spoon, cream the butter and sugar. Add in the eggs, then the flour, baking soda, and salt. Add in the sour cream. Then fold in the bananas and chocolate chips, and mix just until combined.

Pour the batter into the prepared pan. Bake for about 55 minutes, or until the edges are brown and the center is set. Remove the bread from the oven, and cool in the pan for 20 minutes. Remove the bread from the pan, and let cool completely on a wire rack.

CHOCOLATE CHIP BERRY MUFFINS

Tracey Zabar

I make these morning treats every summer when blueberries are in season. Most muffins are traditionally made with melted butter, but I was once distracted by a crying baby while I was making them, and didn't pay attention to my recipe card. They are better, for sure, with the butter creamed instead. The addition of chips and pearls provides a chocolaty crunch to these classic muffins.

• MAKES ABOUT 24 SMALL MUFFINS

1½ cups cake flour

2 teaspoons baking powder

½ teaspoon salt

4 ounces (1 stick) unsalted butter, softened

¾ cup plus 2 tablespoons granulated sugar, divided

1 large egg

¾ cup heavy cream

6 ounces (1 cup) bittersweet chocolate chips

6 ounces (1 cup) Valrhona crunchy pearls

2 cups strawberries, washed and hulled, or blueberries or blackberries, washed and picked over

Preheat the oven to 400°F. Line a mini muffin tin with cupcake papers; set aside.

Into a medium bowl, sift together the cake flour, baking powder, and salt, and set aside.

In the bowl of a stand mixer fitted with the paddle attachment, cream the butter and ¾ cup of the sugar. Add the egg. Add the dry ingredients and cream alternately in two additions each. With a silicone spatula, fold in the chocolate chips, pearls, and berries.

Scoop the batter into the prepared muffin papers, filling them to the top, and sprinkle the remaining 2 tablespoons of sugar on the tops of the muffins. Bake for 20 minutes, or until the muffins' edges are golden brown. Remove the muffins from the oven, and let cool completely in the tin.

CHOCOLATE CHIP BREAKFAST BERRY CAKES

Tracey Zabar

These miniature breakfast cakes became part of my repertoire when I changed a few muffin batter ingredients and placed the berries on top rather than incorporating them into the dough. Baking them in little fluted tart pans makes cakes that are more elegant than muffins. · MAKES 12 SERVINGS

4 ounces (1 stick) unsalted butter, softened, plus more for the pans

2 cups all-purpose flour

2 teaspoons baking powder

½ teaspoon salt

2 cups fresh berries (a combination of blueberries, raspberries, strawberries, and blackberries)

¾ cup granulated sugar

1 large egg

½ cup heavy cream

3 ounces (½ cup) bittersweet chocolate chips

Preheat the oven to 350°F. Butter six small tart pans with removable bottoms. Place the tart pans on a half-sheet pan, lined with parchment paper, and set aside.

In a medium bowl, whisk together the flour, baking powder, and salt, and set aside.

Wash and pick over the berries. Hull the strawberries, cut them into quarters, and set aside.

In the bowl of a stand mixer fitted with the paddle attachment, cream the butter and sugar. Mix in the egg. Alternate adding in the cream and dry ingredients, in three additions each, just until incorporated. With a silicone spatula, fold in the chocolate chips.

Pour the batter into the prepared tart pans. Gently place a few berries in each pan. Bake for 25 to 30 minutes, until the cakes are golden. Remove the half-sheet pan from the oven, and cool for 20 minutes in the tart pans. Remove the cakes from the tart pans, and let cool completely on wire racks.

CHERRY CHOCOLATE CHIP SCONES

Tracy Obolsky of North End Grill

Pastry chef Obolsky told me, "I love making these scones, studded with chocolate chips, because they are not too sweet, and go great with coffee. A morning starts off way better with a scone." · MAKES ABOUT 8 LARGE OR 16 SMALL SCONES

½ cup fresh orange juice

½ cup heavy cream, plus more for
 finishing

1 large egg

Grated zest of 3 oranges (use a
 Microplane)

1½ cups cake flour

1½ cups all-purpose flour, plus more
 for rolling

¾ cup confectioners' sugar, sifted

1 teaspoon kosher salt

1 tablespoon plus 1½ teaspoons baking
 powder

1 cup dried cherries

3 ounces (½ cup) bittersweet or
 semisweet chocolate chips

6 ounces (1½ sticks) unsalted butter,
 cold, cut into ½-inch cubes

Raw sugar, for finishing

In a medium bowl, whisk together the orange juice, ½ cup of the cream, the egg, and the orange zest until smooth, and set aside.

In a large bowl, mix together the cake flour, all-purpose flour, confectioners' sugar, salt, baking powder, cherries, and chocolate chips. Add the butter cubes. Using a bench scraper or your hands, cut in the butter until it is the size of peas. Add the wet ingredients and mix just until incorporated.

On a floured surface, roll the dough 1 inch thick, and cut into 3-inch circles. In an airtight container, place the circles in layers (separate each layer with parchment paper), and put in the refrigerator until they are firm, or overnight.

Preheat the oven to 350°F. Line two half-sheet pans with parchment paper.

Remove the dough circles from the refrigerator and place them on the prepared pans. Brush some cream on the top of each one and sprinkle with raw sugar. Bake for about 16 minutes, rotating the pans halfway through the baking time. Remove the scones from the oven, and cool completely on a wire rack.

CHOCOLATE CHIP BRIOCHE DOUGHNUTS WITH CHOCOLATE CHIP—NUTELLA FUDGE AND ORANGE ZEST

Laurent Tourondel of Brasserie Ruhlmann

Chef Tourondel's heavenly chocolate chip doughnuts are time-consuming to make, but well worth the effort. Besides, your entire house will be perfumed with the scent of the rising dough. Tossed in cinnamon sugar, dusted with confectioners' sugar and orange zest, and served with hot Nutella sauce, they are super indulgent. · MAKES ABOUT 6 DOUGHNUTS

BRIOCHE DOUGH

2 tablespoons whole milk

¼ ounce fresh yeast

1½ cups bread flour

1 tablespoon plus 1 teaspoon granulated sugar

½ teaspoon fine sea salt

1 tablespoon heavy cream

1 tablespoon sour cream

2 large eggs

7 tablespoons butter, softened

6 ounces (1 cup) bittersweet chocolate chips

Heat the milk until it feels warm to the touch (110°F on an instant-read thermometer). Crumble the yeast into the milk, and stir until dissolved.

In the bowl of a stand mixer fitted with the paddle attachment, combine the bread flour, sugar, salt, heavy cream, sour cream, and yeast mixture, and mix on low speed. Add the eggs, and stir until the mixture begins to pull away from the sides of the bowl.

Add the butter and bittersweet chocolate chips, and continue to mix until blended, and a sticky dough forms. Cover the dough with plastic wrap and refrigerate for about 2 hours.

CINNAMON SUGAR

¼ cup packed dark brown sugar

¼ cup granulated sugar

1 teaspoon ground cinnamon

In a shallow bowl, blend the brown sugar, granulated sugar, and cinnamon until well combined, and set aside.

NUTELLA FUDGE SAUCE

1½ ounces (¼ cup) milk chocolate chips

1½ ounces (¼ cup) 66 percent dark chocolate chips

¼ cup Nutella

¼ cup whole milk, or more as needed

In the top of a double boiler, melt the milk chocolate chips, dark chocolate chips, and Nutella, and stir to combine. Add the milk as needed to thin out a bit. Leave this mixture on top of the double boiler under a low flame to keep hot.

DEEP-FRYING DOUGHNUTS

2 quarts vegetable oil

Grated zest of 1 orange

3 tablespoons mini chocolate chips

Confectioners' sugar, for dusting

Remove the dough from the refrigerator, and, with your hands, flatten the dough. Using a rolling pin, carefully roll the dough to a thickness of ¾ inch. Cut out 6 rounds, using a 6-inch round cutter. Using a 1¾-inch round cutter, punch out the centers to form the doughnuts.

Place a platter next to the stove. Heat the oil in an extra-large saucepan to 350°F on a deep-fry thermometer. Fry the doughnuts until they are golden brown, 3 to 4 minutes on each side.

Remove the doughnuts from the oil with a spider or slotted spoon, and quickly toss them in the cinnamon sugar; place on the platter. Cool for a few minutes, then drizzle with hot Nutella Fudge Sauce. Sprinkle orange zest and mini chocolate chips on top of each doughnut. Dust with confectioners' sugar.

WAXMAN HOUSEHOLD CHOCOLATE CHIP PANCAKES

Jonathan Waxman of Barbuto

Chef Waxman's family recipe for these easy-to-make pancakes, with melting chocolate chips, has become my family's new weekend breakfast tradition.

• MAKES ABOUT 12 PANCAKES

½ cup fine organic cornmeal
½ cup whole wheat flour
½ cup organic all-purpose flour
1 teaspoon baking powder
¼ teaspoon sea salt
¼ teaspoon ground cinnamon
¼ teaspoon ground nutmeg
2 ounces (½ stick) unsalted butter,
   plus more for the griddle

4 large eggs
1 cup buttermilk
1 teaspoon pure vanilla extract
6 ounces (1 cup) bittersweet or
   semisweet chocolate chips
Maple syrup or whipped cream,
   for serving

In a medium bowl, sift together the cornmeal, whole wheat flour, all-purpose flour, baking powder, salt, cinnamon, and nutmeg, and set aside.

In a small saucepan, melt the 2 ounces of butter, and set aside.

In a large batter bowl, mix together the eggs, buttermilk, and vanilla. Whisk in the butter, and mix just until combined. Sprinkle in the dry ingredients, and mix just until combined. Fold in the chocolate chips.

Heat the griddle to medium-high, and add a small amount of butter. Pour or spoon the batter onto the griddle. When the pancakes start to bubble and begin to brown on the bottoms, flip them with a spatula, and brown the other sides.

Serve the pancakes with maple syrup or whipped cream.

BUTTERMILK WAFFLES WITH CHOCOLATE CHIPS

Cara Tannenbaum and Andrea Tutunjian of the Institute of Culinary Education

Chefs Tannenbaum and Tutunjian are crazy for nuts. These decadent waffles not only include rich almonds or hazelnuts but also chocolate chips. In my house, we use a Belgian waffle maker to make them extra thick. Thick or thin, these waffles are out of this world. • MAKES ABOUT 7 WAFFLES

1 cup all-purpose flour
1 cup almond flour
2 tablespoons packed light brown
   sugar
2 teaspoons baking powder
½ teaspoon baking soda
¼ teaspoon salt
½ cup sour cream
½ cup buttermilk

½ cup whole milk
2 large eggs
¼ cup canola oil
½ cup coarsely chopped, toasted
   almonds (or hazelnuts)
3 ounces (½ cup) semisweet
   chocolate chips
Confectioners' sugar, for dusting

In a large mixing bowl, stir together the all-purpose flour, almond flour, brown sugar, baking powder, baking soda, and salt.

In a separate bowl, whisk together the sour cream, buttermilk, milk, eggs, and oil. Fold the mixture into the dry ingredients using a silicone spatula, scraping as you fold, just until the dry ingredients are moistened. Fold in the nuts and chocolate chips.

Heat a waffle iron and cook the waffles according to the manufacturer's instructions. Dust with confectioners' sugar. Serve the waffles immediately.

CHOCOLATE CHIP "ELVIS" SANDWICH

Laurent Tourondel of Brasserie Ruhlmann

Chef Tourondel's decadent, gooey sandwiches are a sugar lover's dream come true. Elvis would be thrilled. · MAKES 6 SERVINGS

2¼ cups heavy cream

1½ cups whole milk

1½ teaspoons pure vanilla extract

1¾ cups granulated sugar, divided

3 large eggs

2 large egg yolks

2½ tablespoons orange blossom water

2½ tablespoons bourbon

2 teaspoons grated orange zest

Brioche Pullman loaf, cut into twelve ½-inch-thick slices

1½ cups smooth or chunky peanut butter

6 ounces (1 cup) bittersweet or semisweet chocolate chips

2 bananas, thinly sliced

1½ cups clarified butter, divided

Confectioners' sugar, for dusting

In a medium bowl, whisk together the cream, milk, vanilla, ¾ cup of the granulated sugar, eggs, egg yolks, orange blossom water, bourbon, and orange zest to make the French toast base, and set aside.

Place 6 slices of brioche in a single layer on a work surface. Evenly spread 4 tablespoons of peanut butter on each slice, and top each slice with chocolate chips and enough banana to cover it completely. Make each slice a sandwich by topping it with one of the remaining 6 slices of brioche.

Carefully soak each sandwich in the French toast base for 5 seconds on each side, and transfer to a dripping rack.

Heat a large nonstick sauté pan over medium heat. Coat the bottom of the pan with ¼ cup of the clarified butter (heat the butter, then skim off and discard the foam). Evenly sprinkle about 3 tablespoons of the remaining granulated sugar over the clarified butter, enough to cover the bottom of the pan. Allow the sugar to cook until fully incorporated into the butter, and the mixture becomes fluid, about 1 minute. Place a sandwich in the pan, and continuously move it so that it does not burn. Cook for 5 minutes, or until dark golden brown. Flip the

sandwich, and continue to cook on the other side until golden brown. Remove the sandwich from the pan, and repeat with the remaining sandwiches, adding more clarified butter and granulated sugar, as needed. Slice each sandwich in half and dust with confectioners' sugar.

ACKNOWLEDGMENTS

This book would have a lot of blank pages if not for the kindness and generosity of the chefs, pastry chefs, bakers, teachers, and restaurateurs who shared their favorite chocolate chip recipes with me. I am lucky to have a number of chefs who live within snowball-throwing distance of me, and who let me poke them for help. Thanks to those who baked, delivered, torched, decorated, advised, encouraged, introduced, tasted, invented, enabled, helped me figure it all out, and made these delicious treats, as well as those who sent me chips and other wonderful things, and allowed me to beg and borrow:

Christine Burgin and Lola Wegman, Atlas, Bill, and the dogs; Tanya Bastianich Manuali, Myriam Eberhardt, Georgette Farkas, Kurt Gutenbrunner, Michael McCarty, Danny Meyer, Steve Millington, and Jean-Georges Vongerichten; my teachers at the French Culinary Institute; Dino De Angelis, Avery Griffin, Amy Guittard of Guittard Chocolate Company, Bernard Cohen, Spence Halperin, Selma Gilbert, Mary Hamilton, Jessica Hedison, Mrs. Keegan, Sarah Kosikowski of Valrhona, Amy Ma, Marina Malchin, Hilary Ney, Anne Robichaud, Miss Shacks, the Shapiros, Debbie Teitelbaum, the Zaccaro family (especially John Sr.); and to my fellow baker and troublemaker Alexandra Trower Lindsey. More thanks to Nick Malgieri, my baking guru; to Cara Tannenbaum, Bonnie Slotnick, the FDNY, the Red Sox, and those of you who let me pester you till the cows came home. Yes, you, Dominique Ansel, and Thomas Keller, and you too Johnny Iuzzini. And to Pichet Ong and Sherry Yard, who were gracious enough not to laugh at me when the cake fell.

To my family at Zabar's and Company especially David, Stanley, Saul, and Danny Zabar, for all the bittersweet chips. Thanks to everyone at Rizzoli: I have only ever worked with one editor, Sandy Gilbert, and only ever will. Thank you to my sweet publisher, Charles Miers, and to Maria Pia Gramaglia, Jennifer Pierson, Christopher Steighner, Jono Jarrett, Deborah Weiss Geline, Susan Lynch, Pam Sommers, Jessica Napp, Susan Homer, and Marilyn Flaig. To the rest of my amazing book team: Ellen Silverman, who takes the most lovely, light-washed pictures, and my graphic designer, Jan Derevjanik, who is not only a wiz at making the prettiest books in the world but who also let me help name her oh-so-adorable son, Ziggy.

I could not have done this project without my friend and fellow chef-wrangler, pastry chef Alina Martell Acosta, who takes my breath away with her talent and kindness. An extra shout-out is called for to her equally talented husband, Chef Amador Acosta, the extraordinary Chef Michael White, and everyone in the kitchens at Ai Fiori and Marea, who helped me to translate, test, and decipher recipes.

To the memory of my mother, Mary, and godmother, Eleanor, who taught me to bake all things Sicilian style, and the rest of the Blumenreich and Zabar families. To my cousin Jill Verschleiser, who apparently never eats sugar, but I love her anyway. To my brand-new daughter-in-law, Marki: I am so thrilled to have a baker in the family. And to the outlaws: Cara, Michael, Christina, and Nick. With the most love to my sweet husband, David, and children, Benjamin, Danny, Michael, William, and Mary Rose—this one is for you.

A portion of the proceeds from each book benefits the Women Bake Bread Scholarship Fund at Hot Bread Kitchen, which is a nonprofit organization founded by Jessamyn Rodriguez. Hot Bread Kitchen works with immigrant women and minority entrepreneurs to provide baking, business, and English-language skills and on-the-job training needed to secure careers in the culinary industry, while baking delicious breads from around the world. www.hotbreadkitchen.org

SOURCES

KING ARTHUR FLOUR
135 U.S. Route 5 South
Norwich, Vermont 05055
(800) 827-6836
www.kingarthurflour.com
The Baker's Store for flour, yeast, black cocoa powder, and malt powder.

VALRHONA
www.valrhona-chocolate.com
Baking chocolate, fèves, chocolate and crunchy pearls.

ZABAR'S AND COMPANY, INC.
2245 Broadway
New York, New York 10024
(800) 697-6301
www.zabars.com
The ultimate source for all kinds of kitchen equipment and baking ingredients, including KitchenAid stand mixer and attachments; baking pans and tools; King Arthur flour; Ghirardelli, Valrhona, and Guittard chocolates; Droste Dutch process cocoa powder; nuts; pistachio paste; dried fruits; spices; et cetera.

U.S. AND METRIC CONVERSION CHARTS

All conversions are approximate.

WEIGHT CONVERSIONS

U.S.	METRIC
½ ounce	14 g
1 ounce	28 g
1½ ounces	43 g
2 ounces	57 g
2½ ounces	71 g
3 ounces	85 g
3½ ounces	100 g
4 ounces	113 g
5 ounces	142 g
6 ounces	170 g
7 ounces	200 g
8 ounces	227 g
9 ounces	255 g
10 ounces	284 g
11 ounces	312 g
12 ounces	340 g
13 ounces	368 g
14 ounces	400 g
15 ounces	425 g
1 pound	454 g

OVEN TEMPERATURES

°F	GAS MARK	°C
250	½	120
275	1	140
300	2	150
325	3	165
350	4	180
375	5	190
400	6	200
425	7	220
450	8	230
475	9	240
500	10	260
550	Broil	290

LIQUID CONVERSIONS

U.S.	METRIC
1 teaspoon	5 ml
1 tablespoon	15 ml
2 tablespoons	30 ml
3 tablespoons	45 ml
¼ cup	60 ml
⅓ cup	75 ml
⅓ cup plus 1 tablespoon	90 ml
⅓ cup plus 2 tablespoons	100 ml
½ cup	120 ml
⅔ cup	150 ml
¾ cup	180 ml
¾ cup plus 2 tablespoons	200 ml
1 cup	240 ml
1 cup plus 2 tablespoons	275 ml
1¼ cups	300 ml
1⅓ cups	325 ml
1½ cups	350 ml
1⅔ cups	375 ml
1¾ cups	400 ml
1¾ cups plus 2 tablespoons	450 ml
2 cups (1 pint)	475 ml
2½ cups	600 ml
3 cups	725 ml
4 cups (1 quart)	945 ml
(1,000 ml = 1 liter)	

INDEX

First published in the United States of America in
2015 by Rizzoli International Publications, Inc.
300 Park Avenue South
New York, New York 10010
www.rizzoliusa.com

2015 2016 2017 2018 /
10 9 8 7 6 5 4 3 2 1

Printed in China

ISBN 13: 978-0-7893-2948-6

Library of Congress Control Number: 2015938572

Project Editor: Sandra Gilbert
Graphic design by Jan Derevjanik